FOUR SEASONS WITH ENA

FOUR SEASONS WITH ENA

ENA THOMAS

Photography by John Fry, Swansea

HUGHES

First printed: September 2000

ISBN 0 85284 302 X

Editor: Luned Whelan

Typeset and printed in Wales by:
Gwasg Dinefwr, Rawlings Road,
Llandybïe, Carmarthenshire SA18 3YD

Published by:
Hughes a'i Fab, Parc Tŷ Glas,
Llanisien, Cardiff CF14 5DU

CONTENTS

ACKNOWLEDGEMENTS

I would like to thank the following people for their help in preparing this book: Geoff Thomas, my husband, for his support and his organisation of the recipes; John Fry for his wonderful photographs; the staff at Gwasg Dinefwr Press and Luned Whelan, editor, keen taster and friend.

FOREWORD

The world of food shopping has changed beyond all recognition from the time when I started cooking many years ago. In those days, especially in the country, produce came and went in its season, and those foods that could be preserved were kept in various methods – salting, jams and pickling, for example.

Today, you can buy most produce all year round in supermarkets, but I still believe that food tastes better in season. I have based the recipes in this book on that principle.

I have also made a change to the order of the recipes by arranging them in menus, so that you can choose a whole meal if you wish to do so. Of course, you can use individual dishes at any time of year if it suits you, but when we all lead such busy lives, it may help to have ideas together at your fingertips.

I hope you enjoy preparing and making these recipes – even the more advanced ones can be fun to put together if you like to spend quality time in your kitchen; I know I do!

Iechyd da!

ENA

CONVERSION TABLES

The following are all approximate measurements, which have been either rounded up or down. You should make it a practice that you never mix imperial and metric measurements in any recipe; always adhere to one standard.

MEASUREMENTS

⅛ inch	3mm
¼ inch	5mm
½ inch	1.2cm
1 inch	2.5cm
1¼ inch	3cm
1½ inch	4cm
1¾ inch	4.5cm
2 inch	5cm
2½ inch	6cm
3 inch	7.5cm
3½ inch	9cm
4 inch	10cm
5 inch	13cm
5½ inch	13.5cm
6 inch	15cm
6½ inch	16cm
7 inch	18cm
7½ inch	19cm
8 inch	20cm
9 inch	23cm
9½ inch	24cm
10 inch	25.5cm
11 inch	28cm
12 inch	30cm

VOLUME

2fl oz	55ml
3fl oz	75ml
5fl oz (¼ pint)	150ml
½ pint	275ml
¾ pint	425ml
1 pint	570ml
1½ pints	725ml
1¾ pints	1 litre
2 pints	1.1 litre
2½ pints	1.4 litre
4 pints	2.25 litre

WEIGHTS

½ oz	10g
¾ oz	15g
1 oz	25g
1½ oz	40g
2 oz	50g
2½ oz	65g
3 oz	75g
4 oz	110g
4½ oz	125g
5 oz	150g
6 oz	175g
7 oz	200g
8 oz	225g
9 oz	250g
10 oz	275g
12 oz	350g
1 lb	450g
1½ lb	700g
2 lb	900g
3 lb	1.35kg

OVEN TEMPERATURES

140C	275F	Mark 1
150C	300F	Mark 2
170C	325F	Mark 3
180C	350F	Mark 4
190C	375F	Mark 5
200C	400F	Mark 6
220C	425F	Mark 7
230C	450F	Mark 8
240C	475F	Mark 9

SPRING

The quality of the seasonal ingredients available in Spring seems to reflect the change in season – crisp, clean and fresh tasting. The menus in this chapter make the most of this freshness.

MENUS

Easter Celebration Dinner

Fresh Watercress Soup
Salmon in Puff Pastry
Hollandaise Sauce
Crisp Green Salad/Minted New Potatoes
Poached Pears in Red Wine
Celebration Cake

Spring Brunch

Kedgeree with Carmarthen Ham
Potato and Laverbread Fritters
Tropical Fruit Salad

Mother's Day Breakfast

Orange and Grapefruit Cocktail
Crispy Bacon and Poached Egg Crumpet
Fresh Strawberries

Spring Dinner Party

Potato Gnocchi
Fruity Welsh Lamb with Saffron Rice
Chocolate and Orange Meringue Roulade

Easter Celebration Dinner

FRESH WATERCRESS SOUP

Ingredients
350g/12oz fresh watercress
1 onion, finely chopped
4 green shallots
1 clove crushed garlic
2 large potatoes, peeled and chopped
570ml/1 pint chicken stock
150ml/¼ pint sour cream
a little nutmeg

Method
- Place the onion, the shallots, the garlic, the potatoes and the stock in a heavy-based pan, cover and bring to the boil. Reduce the heat and simmer for 15 minutes.

- Next, add the chopped watercress and simmer for 5 minutes.

- Purée the soup, using a blender or a processor, until it is smooth. Leave to cool.

- Serve with sour cream and grated nutmeg.

SALMON IN PUFF PASTRY

Serves 4-6

This delicious combination of salmon fillet, leeks and asparagus makes a perfect centrepiece for an Easter dinner or on a summer evening. Serve with crispy green salad, new Pembrokeshire potatoes and a Hollandaise sauce.

Ingredients

900g/2lbs salmon fillet, skinned, and all bones removed
450g/1lb puff pastry
225g/8oz leeks, washed and finely sliced
25g /1oz butter
225g/8oz asparagus tips, fresh or tinned

rind and juice of 1 lemon
2 tablespoons freshly chopped parsley
75g /3oz cream cheese
1 beaten egg to glaze
2 tablespoons chopped dill
salt and pepper

Method

- Pre-heat the oven to 200C/400F/Gas 6.

- Roll out half the pastry to a rectangle 1"/2.5 cm larger than the trimmed salmon fillet. Place on a baking tray, prick all over. Cook for about 15 minutes until risen and golden brown, then transfer to a cooling tray.

- Heat the butter in a pan and gently cook the leeks and asparagus for 2-3 minutes. Leave to cool for 2-3 minutes.

- Mix together the cream cheese, the leeks and asparagus, the lemon juice and rind, the parsley, the dill and the seasoning.

- Place the cooled pastry base on to the baking tray. Arrange the salmon fillet on top, with the skin side down. Spoon the cheese mixture over the top.

- Roll out the remaining puff pastry to a larger piece than the salmon fillet, and brush the edges of the cooked pastry with the beaten egg.

- Cover the salmon with the uncooked pastry and neatly tuck the edges under the pastry base. Brush with the beaten egg and gently mark a lattice pattern with a knife over the top.

- Cook in the oven for 25-30 minutes until the pastry is golden brown. When cooked, gently remove on to a serving dish and garnish with a sprig of dill.

- Note: ready-made puff pastry is available at all good supermarkets.

HOLLANDAISE SAUCE

This famous, thick, rich and golden sauce is a perfect partner for fish, eggs, chicken, and for all delicate vegetables, such as asparagus or broccoli and peas.

Makes 275ml / ½ pint. Serves 4 to 6

Ingredients
3 egg yolks
1 tablespoon lemon juice
1 tablespoon cold water
pinch salt and white pepper
175g/6oz unsalted butter, at room temperature

Method
- Place the egg yolks, the lemon juice, the water and a pinch of salt and pepper into a small basin. Rest the basin over a pan of simmering water. The basin should not touch the water.

- With a whisk, beat steadily until the mixture thickens to a smooth cream. Immediately remove the pan and basin from the heat. Now start adding the butter about 25g/1oz at a time and whisk until completely absorbed. Continue adding the butter, whisking in each addition.

- The result should be a creamy sauce of a coating consistency. If it is too thick, thin it by adding a few drops of warm water.

- Note: never allow the sauce to overheat at any stage, or it will become thin and may even curdle!

CRISP GREEN SALAD

Serves 4-6

Ingredients
200g/7oz packet mixed salad leaves
3 tablespoons olive oil
2 cloves garlic, crushed
1 tablespoon white wine vinegar
salt and pepper

Method
- Arrange the salad leaves in a bowl. Place the olive oil, the garlic and the white wine vinegar into a jam jar and shake well. Season with salt and pepper.

- Pour the dressing around the bowl and toss the leaves around. Do this just before serving.

MINTED NEW POTATOES

Serves 4-6

Ingredients
900g/2lbs Pembrokeshire potatoes
4 sprigs fresh mint
50g/2oz butter
3 tablespoons finely chopped mint

Method
- Scrub the potatoes clean, then place into cold salted water with the sprigs of mint and boil for 15-20 minutes until tender.

- Drain the potatoes, discard the mint sprigs, toss in the butter and sprinkle with chopped mint to serve.

POACHED PEARS IN RED WINE

Puddings are a must after a meal. Poached pears with a meringue topping are just delicious.

Ingredients
6 pears
425ml/¾ pint red wine
175g/6oz golden caster sugar
a stick of cinnamon
juice and rind of 1 lemon

The Meringue
4 egg whites
225g/8oz caster sugar
225g/8oz Amaretti biscuits
2 tablespoons Amaretto liqueur

Method
- Peel the pears, cut in half and remove the core. Pour the wine into a shallow saucepan and stir in the sugar, the cinnamon stick, and the juice and rind of the lemon. Bring to the boil, stirring until the sugar has dissolved.

- Place the pears into the wine syrup, cover and poach for 15 minutes.

- Remove from the syrup with a slotted spoon and place into an ovenproof dish. Boil the syrup until it reduces to a thick consistency.

- In a very clean bowl whisk the egg whites until stiff, then gradually beat in the sugar. Beat until the meringue is glossy.

- Crush the biscuits into large pieces and mix into the meringue with the liqueur. Pile the meringue onto the pears.

- Place into the oven and cook for 15-20 minutes at 180C/350F/Gas 4 until golden brown.

- To serve, divide into 4-6 portions and pour the sauce around each one.

- Variations: peaches, plums, apples or any summer fruits can be used. Into the meringue you can add walnuts, pecan nuts, chocolate drops or creamed coconut. Tip: always choose fruit which are ripe but firm.

CELEBRATION CAKE

Easter is a time when we feel like making something special. Why not try this delicious spicy almond cake, which is a little different from the traditional simnel cake. Children would probably prefer this cake because of the tempting chocolate topping.

Ingredients
225g/8oz unsalted butter
225g/8oz soft brown sugar
4 eggs
275g/10oz self-raising flour
50g/2oz ground almonds
rind of 1 lemon
rind and juice of 1 orange
½ teaspoon ground coriander
½ teaspoon ground cloves
1 teaspoon ground ginger
1 teaspoon cinnamon
225g/8oz marzipan

Fudge Topping
225g/8oz icing sugar
50g/2oz cocoa powder
3 tablespoons double cream
75g/3oz caster sugar
75g/3oz butter

To decorate
Physalis (Cape gooseberry)
Easter chicks and eggs
edible gold powder

Method
- Grease and line a 23cm/9" cake tin.

- Cream together the butter and sugar until light and fluffy. Beat in the eggs one at a time.

- Sieve the flour and spices and fold into the creamy mixture with the ground almonds, the lemon rind, and the rind and juice of the orange.

- Roll out the marzipan to a 20cm/8" round, using a little icing sugar on the rolling pin and the work surface.

- Spoon half the cake mixture into the prepared cake tin. Place the marzipan on top, then spoon the remaining cake mixture on top and even out with a palette knife.

- Cook in a preheated oven at 150C/300F/Gas 2 for 1¼ hours. The cake should be firm to touch. Leave to cool for about 15 minutes, then turn onto a cooling tray.

- To make the fudge topping: sieve the cocoa and icing sugar into a mixing bowl.

- Place the butter, the cream and the caster sugar into a saucepan, and gently heat until the butter and sugar have melted, then boil for 1 minute.

- Pour the mixture into the icing sugar and cocoa, and beat well until smooth.

- Spread over the cooled cake and decorate with Easter eggs, chicks, and physalis. Paint the leaves of the physalis with edible gold powder.

- Note: edible gold powder is available from most good cookshops. Physalis is just heaven to eat, and is available in most supermarkets.

Spring Brunch

KEDGEREE WITH CARMARTHEN HAM

Serves 6

Ingredients

350g/12oz Basmati and wild rice
1 large onion, finely chopped
2 teaspoons ground coriander
2 teaspoons ground cumin
1 tablespoon chopped parsley
1 tablespoon chopped coriander
salt and pepper

725ml/1½ pints chicken stock or water
275ml/½ pint *crème fraîche*
700g/1½ lbs smoked cod, haddock or salmon
225g/8oz Carmarthen ham
1 tablespoon olive oil
50g/2oz butter

Method

- In a large pan, gently heat the oil and butter. Add the spices and the onion and cook until the onion is translucent. Add the rice and cook for 1-2 minutes.

- Pour in the stock, stir well and bring to the boil. Cover and cook over a low heat for 15-20 minutes until all the stock has been absorbed. Stir occasionally.

- Place the fish in a shallow pan with a little water, cover and cook over a low heat for 10 minutes, or microwave for 5 minutes on full power, using a suitable microwave dish.

- Remove the fish from the pan, and flake into large pieces.

- Fry the Carmarthen ham in a little hot oil until crisp and curled up slightly. Drain on kitchen paper.

- To assemble the kedgeree: place the rice into a large serving bowl, gently fold in the fish, the *crème fraîche*, the herbs and seasoning, together with the Carmarthen ham.

- Tip: if you wish to make it the day before, cover and chill in the refrigerator. Then the following day place a little oil or knob of butter on top, and cover with foil. Warm through in a pre-heated oven at 150C/300F/Gas 2 for 15-20 minutes.

- Serve with Potato and Laverbread Fritters.

POTATO AND LAVERBREAD FRITTERS

I had a wonderful experience when I visited St. David's in Pembrokeshire recently. Two very dear local ladies took me to White Sands to collect seaweed off the rocks during low tide. Having gathered a basketful, we took it back to their home, and washed it well, then boiled it for 6 hours, and finally drained and chopped it.

I then proceeded to make the following recipe. But who were the two ladies? They were Edna Morgan, aged 93, and Eunice Smith, aged 90. Well done to both of you!

Ingredients
225g/8oz cooked mashed potatoes
110g/4oz laverbread
50g/2oz plain flour
50g/2oz oatmeal
2 eggs, beaten
150ml/¼ pint single cream
1 teaspoon mixed herbs
225g/8oz streaky bacon
salt and pepper

Method
- Place the mashed potato into a large bowl, stir in the flour and the oatmeal and mix well.

- Pour in the beaten eggs, the cream, the herbs and the salt and pepper, and the prepared laverbread. Mix well.

- Heat a little oil in a non-stick frying pan, and drop a teaspoonful of the mixture at a time into the hot pan. Leave for 1-2 minutes, then turn over with a palette knife.

- Cook for one more minute on both sides until golden brown.

- Fry the bacon and serve with the fritters. This makes a delicious breakfast with grilled tomatoes.

- Laverbread is a Welsh delicacy, equivalent to caviar in my opinion.

TROPICAL FRUIT SALAD

Serves 4

Ingredients
3 ripe mangoes
225g/8oz fresh pineapple
4 kiwi fruits
50g/2oz physalis (Cape gooseberries)
2 papayas
50g/2oz caster sugar
grated rind and juice of 1 lemon
2 pieces preserved stem ginger in syrup
150ml/¼ pint ginger wine
450g/1lb lychees, fresh or canned

Method

- Place the sugar, the lemon juice and rind and 150ml/¼ pint of water into a saucepan and bring to the boil. Finely chop the preserved ginger and stir into the syrup. Leave to cool.

- To prepare the fruit: peel the lychees, cut in half and remove the stone. Peel the mangoes and cut the flesh away from the stone, then cut into cubes. Peel and slice the kiwi, peel the papaya and cut in half, then remove the seeds and cut into cubes. Peel and slice the pineapple and remove the core, then cut into cubes.

- Place all the fruit into a large glass serving bowl and pour the syrup over. Cover with clingfilm and chill for a few hours. Decorate with the physalis.

Mother's Day Breakfast

Mother's Day gives children the oportunity to prepare a delicious breakfast to spoil their mother (with an adult to 'help' them if they're very young). Then all the family can make a special effort to sit around the table together to celebrate this occasion. Place bowls of fresh strawberries on the table, to be eaten before or after the savoury dish.

ORANGE AND GRAPEFRUIT COCKTAIL   Serves 4

Fresh fruit cocktail is refreshing, simple to make, and very healthy to eat.

Ingredients
2 oranges
2 pink grapefruit
4 cocktail cherries
small bunch of chopped chives
2 passion fruit

Method
- Cut the top and bottom peel off the oranges and grapefruit, then with a sharp knife remove all the peel and pith.

- Cut between each segment of orange and grapefruit, leaving you with just the fruit segments, without the skin. Doing this makes it so much easier to eat.

- Divide the fruit between four glass dishes, sprinkle over the chives and decorate with a cocktail cherry, then cut the passion fruit in half and scatter the pulpy seeds over the fruit.

CRISPY BACON AND POACHED EGG CRUMPET

Ingredients

4 crumpets
8 slices thinly cut rindless streaky bacon
4 fresh eggs

450g/1lb cherry tomatoes
juice of 1 lemon
a few sprigs of parsley

Method

- Pop the crumpets under the grill to toast, and keep them warm.

- Heat a little oil in a frying pan and fry the bacon until crispy and golden brown, then keep it warm. Cut the tomatoes in half and fry in the bacon fat.

- Lightly poach the eggs in simmering water with lemon juice for 2-3 minutes.

- To assemble: on warm plates, place the poached egg on top of the crumpet, and wrap the bacon slices around the crumpet. Place the tomatoes next to each crumpet. Garnish with parsley.

Alternative:

SCRAMBLED EGGS
WITH SMOKED SALMON   **Serves 4**

Ingredients

6 eggs
4 tablespoons double cream
salt and pepper
50g/2oz butter
110g/4oz smoked salmon

Method

- Whisk the eggs and cream together and season with a little salt and black pepper.

- In a non-stick saucepan, heat the butter, then pour in the egg mixture and stir over a low heat until all the egg is cooked and scrambled (1-2 minutes). Now cut the salmon into small pieces and toss into the scrambled eggs.

- Serve on a round of toast or a fresh bread roll cut in half, or on a crumpet and sprinkle over some chopped parsley.

POTATO GNOCCHI

Serves 4 (as a starter)
Serves 2 (as a main course)

Gnocchi is a very much an Italian dish, but I am going to give it a Welsh flavour, using some Welsh produce.

Ingredients
900g/2lbs old floury potatoes such as King Edward or Maris Piper
pinch of salt
50g/2oz Welsh butter
1 beaten egg
225g/8oz plain flour

Sauce 1
110g/4oz Carmarthen Ham
50g/2oz button mushrooms
1 clove crushed garlic
1 tablespoon chopped parsley or basil
2 tablespoons olive oil
2 chopped plum tomatoes
50g/2oz Gorgonzola cheese

Sauce 2
225g/8oz laverbread
110g/4oz cockles
1 small onion,finely chopped
275ml/½ pint double cream
juice of ½ lemon
salt and pepper to season
1 tablespoon olive oil

Method
- Cook the potatoes in their skin in boiling water for about 20 minutes. Drain well, then cool slightly. While the potatoes are still warm, remove the skins, and mash well or push them through a sieve into a bowl.

- Season with salt and pepper, add the butter, the egg and half the flour. Mix well to bind.

- Turn the mixture on to a floured surface and knead, gradually adding more flour until the dough is soft, smooth and slightly sticky.

- With floured hands, roll the dough into thin ropes. Cut into 1.7cm/¾ inch pieces. Press a finger into each piece of dough to flatten, then draw your finger towards you to curl the sides of the gnocchi, or use a fork. Spread the gnocchi on a floured tea towel.

- Gently cook the gnocchi in batches, in a pan of simmering water for 2-3 minutes at a time, until they float to the surface. Remove from the water and keep warm on a serving plate.

- To make Sauce 1: heat the oil in a pan, fry the onion and the mushrooms for 1-2 minutes, then add the chopped ham, the garlic, the chopped tomato and the parsley.

- Simmer for 2 minutes, add the Gorgonzola and cook until the cheese starts to melt, then mix in the parsley and the basil. Spoon it over the gnocchi.

- To make Sauce 2: heat the oil in a pan and fry the chopped onion, then add the cockles, the laverbread, the lemon juice and the seasoning.

- Pour in the cream and just bring to the boil. Spoon it over the gnocchi.

- Tip: the gnocchi dough can be made and shaped in advance, and frozen. They can be cooked from frozen.

FRUITY WELSH LAMB
WITH SAFFRON RICE

Serves 4

This recipe is given a slight twist by using Welsh lamb. An ideal dish to make and freeze for a buffet, or to warm yourself up on a cold winter night.

Ingredients
700g /1½lb Welsh lamb, leg or shoulder
1 teaspoon ground cumin
1 teaspoon garam masala
1 teaspoon thyme
75 ml/3fl oz fresh orange juice
50g/2oz large raisins
110g/4oz ready-to-eat apricots
150ml/5fl oz brandy or sherry
50g/2oz plain flour
salt and pepper to taste
3 shallots
1 teaspoon ground coriander
½ teaspoon ground cloves
2 cloves garlic
1 teaspoon saffron threads
55ml/2fl oz sherry vinegar
275ml/½ pint lamb stock
2 tablespoons olive oil

Saffron Rice
225g/8oz arborio or carnaroli
    rice
50g/2oz butter
1 tablespoon olive oil
1 medium onion,
    finely chopped
725ml/1½ pints chicken stock
pinch of saffron threads
1 lemon, rind and juice
salt and pepper
1 tablespoon chopped parsley

Method
- Soak the raisins and the apricots for 3-4 hours in the brandy or sherry and the orange juice.

- Cut the lamb into bite-size pieces, then toss in the flour.

- Heat the oil in a large pan and fry the lamb until brown all over. Now add the spices, the shallots and the garlic and cook for 2-3 minutes.

- Pour in the stock and add the vinegar and the soaked fruit, and bring to the boil. Spoon the lamb into a casserole dish, cover and cook in the oven for about 1¼ hours at 180C/350F/Gas 4. Remove from the oven and taste for seasoning.

- To make the saffron rice: heat the oil and butter in a large saucepan, stir in the chopped onion and cook until soft. Add the rice and stir into the onion, pour in some stock and keep stirring. Then add more stock, and after about 15 minutes the rice should start to thicken.

- Stir the saffron and the lemon juice into the rice. Cook for a further 5 minutes.

- The consistency of the rice should not be dry or too wet, but just a nice creamy consistency. Stir in the parsley and some toasted flaked almonds.

- Note: if the rice is too dry, add a little extra stock. Leeks or mushrooms can also be added to the lamb.

CHOCOLATE AND ORANGE MERINGUE ROULADE

This recipe is a firm favourite with most people, and is ideal when you are planning a family and friends' get-together. It is also great to freeze.

Ingredients
5 large egg whites
275g/10oz caster sugar
50g/2oz finely chopped pistachio nuts

The Filling
425ml/¾ pint double cream
1 orange, in segments, without the membrane
1 tablespoon orange liqueur
225g/8oz good quality chocolate

Method
- Line a Swiss roll tin 33cm x 23cm/13" x 9" with parchment paper.

- Whisk the egg whites in a clean bowl until firm. To test if ready to add the sugar – it should not slide around the bowl. Gradually beat in the sugar until thick and glossy. Spoon the meringue into the prepared tin and gently spread it evenly.

- Sprinkle the nuts over the meringue. Bake for 8 minutes in a pre-heated fan oven at 180C/350F/Gas 4, then reduce the temperature for a further 10-15 minutes at 150C/300F/Gas 2. The meringue should be golden and firm to touch.

- Remove the meringue from the oven, and turn out on to a sheet of baking parchment. Remove the lining paper from the meringue and allow to cool for about 10 minutes.

- Whisk the cream until thick, and mix in the liqueur. Spread the cream over the meringue and, using the parchment, roll up the meringue (it will crack, as it should).

- Decorate with piped cream and orange segments on top, then melt the chocolate, and drizzle it over the roulade – be as artistic as you like!

- To freeze the roulade, do not decorate. Open-freeze it quickly, then wrap in foil before returning it to the freezer. Remove it 3-4 hours before decorating and serving it as above.

SUMMER

Eating outside is one of the great pleasures of summer – in the sun or in the shade, around a table or on a blanket, it's hard to beat! If the weather doesn't co-operate, any of the dishes in this chapter are equally delicious eaten in the comfort of your home!

MENUS

Picnic Time

Ham and Potato Whirls
Ena's Corned Beef Pies
with a Difference
Welsh Eggs
Turkey Meatloaf with Tomato Sauce
Salmon and Broccoli Terrine
Carrot Cake with Prune Purée

Barbecue Time

Dips
Prawns in Carmarthen Ham
Spicy Mackerel
Minced Turkey Patties
Spicy Beefburgers with Melted Cheese
Welsh Beef with Melon and Mint Salad
Warm Barbecue Pudding

Vegetarian Dinner Party

Blue Cheese and Chive Balls
Roast Peppers with Courgette Curry
Carrot and Herb Roulade
Banana and Mango Mousse

Summer Buffet

Salmon and Leek Tart
Summer Curried Chicken with Melon and Tomato Salad
Spicy Vegetables with Couscous
Garlic Potato Salad
Summer Puddings with Raspberry and Blackcurrant Sauce
Rhubarb and Orange Meringue Flan

Summer Celebration

Pan Grilled Scallops with Pepper Sauce
Roasted Boned Chicken with Duck Breasts and Stuffing
Cox's Apple Pudding with Real Custard

Picnic Time

These picnic recipes have been selected for taste and convenience. All the dishes can be prepared in advance, and several can be frozen or stored in case the weather lets you down! You can make the picnic formal, with china, glass and cutlery, or pitch in with your fingers, using colourful plastic crockery.

HAM AND POTATO WHIRLS

Children and adults alike will simply love these whirls, made with puff pastry, which you can buy in most food stores, saving you preparation time.

Ingredients
450g/1lb cooked mashed potatoes
225g/8oz minced cooked ham
1 finely chopped onion
2 tablespoons chopped parsley
salt and pepper to taste
450g/1lb ready-made puff pastry
1 beaten egg

Method
- Mix together the potatoes, the ham, the onion, the parsley and the seasoning.
- Roll out the pastry to an oblong 30cm x 20cm/12" x 8". Spread the potato filling all over it, then brush the edges with the egg.
- Roll the pastry up as if you were rolling a Swiss roll, then brush with the remaining egg, and cut the roll into 10 slices. Place on a baking tray and cook in a hot oven at 200C/400F/Gas 6 for about 20 minutes until the pastry is golden brown and crisp.
- Serve with a crisp green salad, and a dressing made by placing the following ingredients in a jar and shaking well: 3 tablespoons olive oil; 1 tablespoon lemon juice; 1 tablespoon chopped chives and 1 tablespoon balsamic vinegar. Keep the dressing in the jar until required.
- Grated cheese, corned beef, chicken and turkey can be used instead of ham. Also tinned salmon or tuna can be used.
- Tip: you can prepare a large quantity of these whirls and freeze them uncooked, then cook from frozen, as required.

ENA'S CORNED BEEF PIES WITH A DIFFERENCE

These tasty little pies are as easy to pack for a picnic as they are to eat!

Makes 6 small or 1 large pie

Ingredients
Cheese and chive pastry
450g/1lb strong flour
110g/4oz butter
110g/4oz white vegetable fat
pinch cayenne pepper
110g/4oz grated Cheddar cheese
bunch of chives, chopped
1 beaten egg

The Filling
350g/12oz tin of corned beef
2 tablespoons redcurrant jelly
1 red onion, finely chopped
2 large tomatoes, seeds and skin removed
salt and pepper

Method
- To make the pastry: place the flour in a bowl, cut the fat into pieces and rub into the flour until it resembles fine breadcrumbs.
- To the mixture, add the cayenne pepper, the cheese and the chives.
- Mix to a soft but firm dough with a little cold water. Chill for ½ an hour.
- Mash the corned beef with a fork, then add the redcurrant jelly, the onion, the tomatoes, and salt and pepper to taste.
- Roll out the pastry fairly thinly, and cut into rounds to fit your greased patty tins or muffin tins.
- Line the tins with the pastry then divide the corned beef mixture between them.
- Roll out the remaining pastry and, with a pastry cutter which fits your patty tins, cut out 6 circles. Place one on each patty; brush with a beaten egg and cook for 15-20 minutes at 200C/400F/Gas 6.

WELSH EGGS

This recipe was sent to me by S. M. Richards from Machynlleth. She used to make them for school children, who really loved them, and apparently they haven't been available in any recipe book until now. In this version, I've added a few extra ingredients such as parsley, chives, and egg yolks to her idea.

Ingredients
4 hard boiled eggs with the shells removed
700g/1½ lb potatoes
salt and pepper
1 tablespoon chopped parsley
1 tablespoon chopped chives
2 egg yolks
½ teaspoon nutmeg
50g/2oz butter
olive oil for frying

To Coat
50g/2oz plain flour
175g/6oz white breadcrumbs
2 eggs, beaten

Method
- Peel the potatoes and boil for about 15-20 minutes until tender. Drain, then mash, mixing in the butter, the nutmeg, the egg yolks, the parsley, the chives, salt and pepper.
- Leave to cool slightly, as this makes the mixture easier to mould around the eggs.
- Mould the potato mixture around the eggs, then toss them first in the flour, then the egg and then the breadcrumbs. Leave in the fridge for about 1 hour.
- Heat the olive oil in a heavy pan, insert the eggs and fry until golden brown and crisp all over. Remove from the oil and drain on kitchen paper.
- Tip: when cooking these for a meal at home rather than for a picnic, serve hot with braised leeks.

TURKEY MEATLOAF WITH TOMATO SAUCE

Ingredients
450g/1lb minced turkey breast
1 onion, peeled and chopped
1 clove garlic, peeled and chopped
1 red pepper, de-seeded and chopped
1 yellow pepper, de-seeded and chopped
1 small red chilli
1 tablespoon fresh thyme
110g/4oz white breadcrumbs
1 beaten egg
2 tablespoons chopped parsley
2 tablespoons chopped coriander
3 tablespoons mango chutney

Tomato Sauce
2 tablespoons olive oil
1 chopped onion
1 clove crushed garlic
225g/8oz cherry tomatoes
1 teaspoon sugar
1 tablespoon tomato purée
1 large red chilli, de-seeded and chopped
150ml/¼ pint white wine

Method

- Grease and line a 700g/1½lb loaf tin with parchment paper. Place all the meatloaf ingredients into a bowl and mix well. Season to taste.

- Spoon into the prepared tin, cover with foil and place in a roasting tin half-filled with water.

- Cook for about 50 minutes at 180C/350F/Gas 4.

- To make the sauce: cut the cherry tomatoes in half. Heat the oil in a saucepan and gently fry the onion, the garlic and the chilli for 2-3 minutes.

- Add the tomatoes, the purée, the sugar and the wine, and boil for about 5 minutes. Use hot or cold and keep in a jar in the fridge. Use only for a picnic for adults unless you like red-stained children!

- Tip: this loaf is ideal for freezing. Remove from the freezer the day before it is needed.

SALMON AND BROCCOLI TERRINE

Serves 6-8

Ingredients
700g/1½ lbs skinned salmon fillets
450g/1lb plaice fillets
1 teaspoon sea salt and black pepper, mixed
350ml/12 fl oz *crème fraîche*
3 tablespoons tartare sauce
4 tablespoons seafood sauce
1 tablespoon chopped parsley
1 tablespoon chopped chives **or** spring onions
150ml/¼ pint white wine
225g/8oz pack of gravalax **or** 225g/8oz pack of smoked salmon
225g /8oz broccoli florets
juice of 1 lemon

You will need a 900g/2lb loaf tin or terrine mould lined with clingfilm

Method
- Place the salmon fillets in a saucepan with a little white wine and lemon juice, cover and poach for 5-8 minutes. Do the same with the plaice fillets.
- Drain the salmon and lift into a bowl. Repeat the process with the plaice, keeping them in separate bowls.
- To the salmon, add some seasoning, 225g/8oz of the *crème fraîche*, 3 tablespoons of the seafood sauce, 2 tablespoons of the tartare sauce, and mix well until smooth – a food processor could be used.
- With a fork, roughly mix the plaice with the remaining tartare sauce, the *crème fraîche*, the seafood sauce and the herbs. This will have a rough texture.
- Steam the broccoli for 5-8 minutes and roughly chop. To assemble the terrine, first line the terrine dish with the gravalax or smoked salmon.
- Place half the salmon mixture into the terrine, top with the plaice mixture then the finely chopped broccoli. Finish with the remaining salmon mixture. Fold over the ends of the smoked salmon or gravalax. Cover with foil and chill for 2-3 days or freeze. If frozen, remove from the freezer the night before eating. Cut into slices before packing it in the picnic basket!

Mother's Day Breakfast: Spring (p. 20).

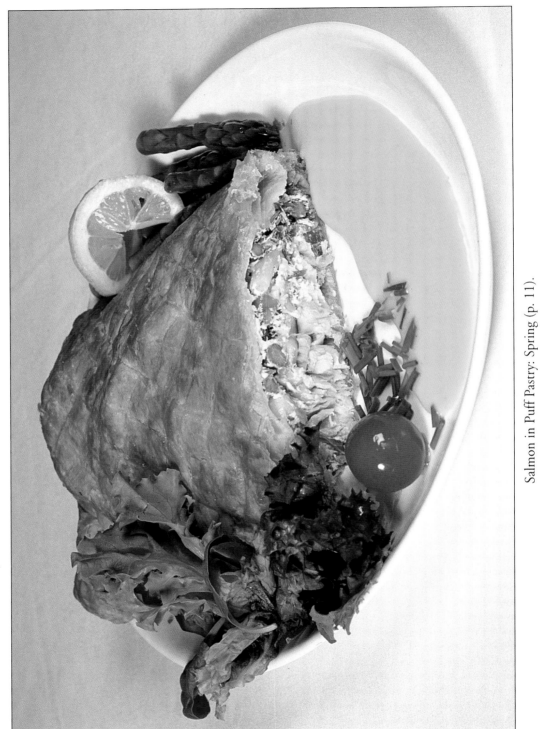

Salmon in Puff Pastry: Spring (p. 11).

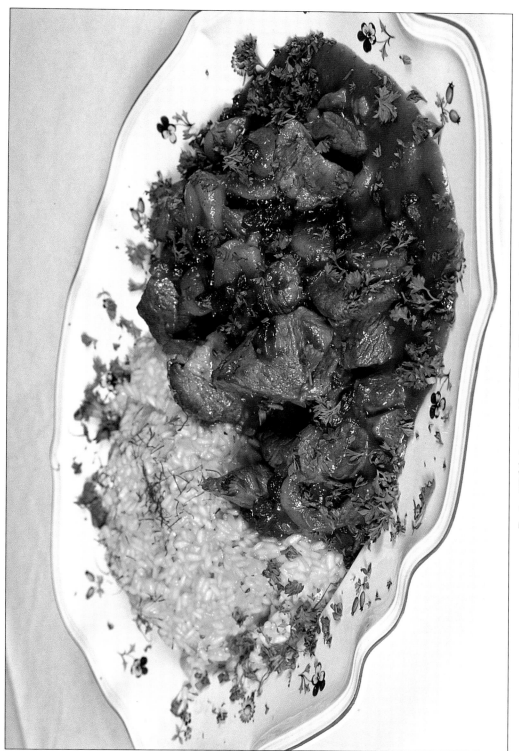

Fruity Welsh Lamb with Saffron Rice: Spring (p. 24).

Chocolate and Orange Meringue Roulade: Spring (p. 26).

Picnic time – l-r: Carrot Cake with Prune Purée; Ham and Potato Whirls;
Ena's Corned Beef Pies with a Difference; Salmon and Broccoli Terrine: Summer (pp. 28-33).

Carrot and Herb Roulade: Summer (p. 46).

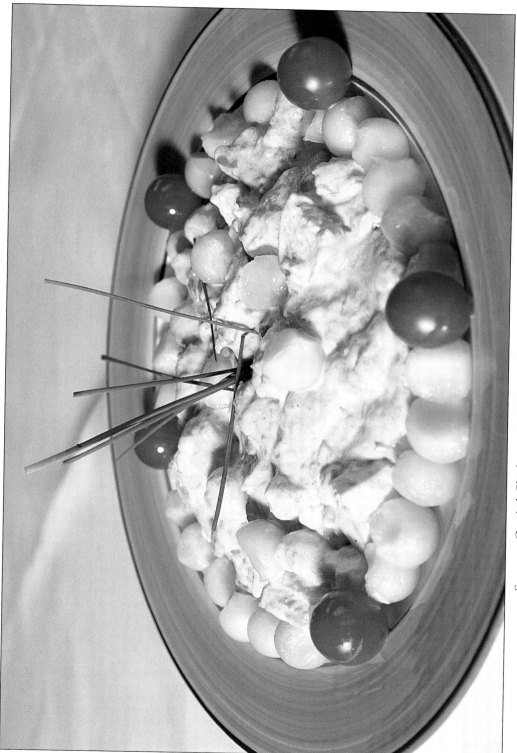

Summer Curried Chicken with Melon and Tomato Salad: Summer (p. 51).

Pan Grilled Scallops with Pepper Sauce: Summer (p. 56).

CARROT CAKE WITH PRUNE PURÉE

This recipe for a very popular cake has been tried and tested by family and friends, especially the editor of this book, who enjoyed it so much she chose it as a wedding cake! Try your favourite topping as a change.

Ingredients
225g/8oz soft brown sugar
225g/8oz unsalted butter
4 eggs
225g/8oz self-raising flour
50g/2oz ground almonds
150g/5oz prune purée
350g/12oz grated carrots
juice and rind of 1 lemon
rind of 1 orange
1 teaspoon baking powder

Topping
225g/8oz cream cheese
rind of 1 orange and 1 lemon
25g/1oz icing sugar

Method
- Grease and line a 20cm/8" round cake tin.
- Peel and coarsely grate the carrots.
- In a large bowl, cream the butter and sugar until light and creamy. Then beat in the eggs one at a time. Stir in the prune purée.
- Fold in the flour, the ground almonds, the baking powder and half the orange and lemon rinds.
- Gently stir in the grated carrots and the lemon juice.
- Spoon into the prepared cake tin and cook for 1¼ hours at 150C/300F/ Gas 2. Leave to cool in the tin, then turn out onto a cooling tray.
- To make the topping: mix together the cream cheese, and the remaining rinds. When the cake is completely cold, spread over the top. At this point you could sprinkle over some chopped walnuts or pistachio nuts.

Barbecue Time

Every summer, we wait optimistically for the weather to allow us to light our barbecues and let the men loose on the coals! These recipes have been collected in hope, and are ideal for men to start the process that leads to firelighters and eating! Whatever your main courses, make sure there's plenty of fresh bread to mop up the juices, and as many fresh salads as you've time to make.

DIPS

Served with crisp raw vegetables, dips are great to get your tastebuds going whilst waiting for the barbecue. Use carrots, celery, green, red and yellow peppers, cucumber, cauliflower and broccoli florets, radishes, and mushrooms cut into manageable pieces, and garlic potato wedges, corn chips or crackers.

CREAMY SMOKED OYSTER AND CHEESE DIP

Ingredients
2 x 75g/3 oz cans smoked oysters
200g/7oz cream cheese
2 tablespoons lemon juice
2 tablespoons chopped chives
50g/2oz chopped sun-dried tomatoes
salt and pepper

Method
- Drain the oysters, place into a food processor with the cream cheese and lemon juice, and process for one minute until smooth.
- Place the mixture into a bowl and mix in the chopped tomatoes and chives. Season to taste.

CANNELLINI BEAN AND ANCHOVY DIP

Ingredients
400g/14 oz can cannellini beans
2 crushed garlic cloves
5 tablespoons olive oil
4 tablespoons lemon juice
8 anchovy fillets
1 tablespoon tomato purée
2 tablespoons fresh chopped parsley and chives

Method
- Place the beans, the garlic, the olive oil, the lemon juice, the tomato purée, and the anchovy fillets into a food processor and process until smooth.
- Season and transfer into a bowl and top with the chives and parsley.

CREAM CHEESE DIP

Ingredients
225g/8oz cream cheese
1 tablespoon chopped chives
1 tablespoon chopped parsley
1 tablespoon chopped basil
3 tablespoons chopped mayonnaise
2 finely chopped shallots
1 clove crushed garlic
juice of ½ lemon
½ teaspoon cayenne pepper

Method
- Blend all the ingredients together, and season to taste.

CORN AND CHIVE DIP

Ingredients
250g/9oz corn relish
350g/12oz sour cream
few drops Tabasco sauce
bunch of chopped fresh chives
50g/2oz grated mature Cheddar cheese

Method
- Combine all ingredients together and gently heat in a saucepan. Do not boil, just stir until the cheese melts. Serve with corn chips.

TOMATO DIP

Ingredients
1 large tomato
2 spring onions
1 small red onion
1 tablespoon chopped mint
1 tablespoon white vinegar
1 clove crushed garlic

Method
- Remove the skin off the tomato by plunging into boiling water for a minute. Cut in half, remove seeds and chop roughly.
- Finely chop the spring onions and red onion.
- Combine all the ingredients and mix well.

AVOCADO DIP

Ingredients
1 large ripe avocado
grated rind and juice of ½ a lemon
110g/4oz full fat cream cheese
2 spring onions
1 clove garlic
season with ground black pepper

Method
- Mix all the ingredients together in a food processor.

- Place in a bowl and chill before serving.

MANGO DIP

Ingredients
1 large ripe mango
2 tablespoons Greek yogurt
pinch five spice powder

Method
- Remove the mango from the big stone and cut away the flesh.

- Place into a food processor, and process until the mango is pulpy.

- Mix the mango and the yogurt together.

- Sprinkle the spice powder over the mixture.

PRAWNS IN CARMARTHEN HAM

Ingredients
6 slices of Carmarthen ham
6 uncooked king prawns

Method
- Remove the shells from the prawns, slit down the back and remove the black, thread-like vein.
- Place each prawn on a slice of Carmarthen ham and roll up.
- Place on to skewers and grill them on the barbecue.

SPICY MACKEREL

Ingredients
4 cleaned mackerel
2 cloves finely chopped garlic
1 teaspoon sea salt
1 teaspoon minced ginger
½ teaspoon ground turmeric
½ teaspoon ground black pepper
1½ teaspoons ground chilli
juice and rind of 1 lemon
5 tablespoons groundnut oil
2 small de-seeded red bell peppers, cut into strips
fresh coriander or parsley to garnish

Method
- Rinse the cleaned fish under cold water and pat dry with kitchen paper.

- Place the garlic, the salt, the ginger, the turmeric, the peppers, the chilli and two tablespoons of the lemon juice into a food processor. Process until smooth.

- Rub the mixture over the fish inside and out, then leave to marinade for 30 minutes.

- Wrap the fish in foil and place on to the barbecue and cook for 5 minutes on both sides.

- Other fish can be used, e.g. trout, sardines or salmon.

MINCED TURKEY PATTIES

Ingredients
450g/1lb minced turkey
110g/4oz fresh white breadcrumbs
1 tablespoon chopped parsley
1 tablespoon chopped thyme
1 tablespoon whole grain mustard
1 clove garlic
1 tablespoon lemon juice and the rind of 1 lemon
salt and pepper to taste
1 beaten egg
1 bunch finely chopped spring onions
4 tablespoons extra virgin olive oil

Tomato Sauce
1 tablespoon extra virgin olive oil
1 finely chopped onion
1 finely chopped carrot
400g/14oz tin chopped tomatoes
1 tablespoon Worcestershire sauce
1 clove crushed garlic
1 tablespoon chopped basil and coriander
150ml/¼ pint apple juice

Method
- In a large mixing bowl, combine the ingredients for the patties. Season and mix together until well blended.

- Divide into 6-8 patties and mould into a flat round, 2.5cm/1" in thickness. Chill before cooking – this makes cooking far easier.

- Place the patties on a hot barbecue and cook for 4-5 minutes on both sides until golden brown and cooked through.

- The sauce can be prepared beforehand. To make the sauce: heat a little oil in a saucepan and fry the onion, the carrot and the garlic for 2-3 minutes.

- Pour in the tomatoes, the apple juice, the Worcestershire sauce and the herbs. Bring to the boil and simmer for 10 minutes. You should now have a delicious, thick sauce.

- Garnish with parsley and orange rind.

SPICY BEEFBURGERS WITH MELTED CHEESE

Serves 6

Ingredients
450g/1lb minced beef
1 finely chopped onion
110g/4oz fresh breadcrumbs
1 tablespoon chopped parsley
1 teaspoon red curry paste
1 tablespoon sun-dried tomato paste
pinch of salt
6 slices of Welsh Cheddar cheese
1 egg
2 tablespoons olive oil

Method
- Place all the ingredients into a bowl and mix well together. Divide into 6 portions.

- Brush the barbecue with a little oil and cook the burgers for 3-4 minutes on both sides.

- When cooked, place on a sheet of foil, and place a slice of cheese over each.

- Place back on the barbecue until the cheese has melted slightly.

WELSH BEEF WITH MELON AND MINT SALAD

A delightful way of serving steaks, with the pungent flavour of orange, elderflower wine and honey. They can be barbecued, grilled or fried.

Ingredients
4 thin sirloin steaks
2 cloves garlic
2 oranges
1 tablespoon white wine vinegar
150ml/¼ pint elderflower wine (Cwmderi or other)
3 tablespoons clear honey
1 tablespoon olive oil

The Salad
half a watermelon
2 avocados
bunch of spring onions
bunch of chopped mint
salt and pepper

Method
- Cut the garlic into thin slivers and insert all over the steaks.

- Make a marinade with the rind and juice of the oranges, the wine, the vinegar, the honey and the oil. Immerse the steaks into the marinade, cover and refrigerate for 2-3 hours.

- To make the salad, remove the seeds and skin of the melon. Cut into bite-size pieces. Cut the avocados in half, remove the stones and peel; cut into bite-size pieces.

- Chop the spring onions. Mix all the salad together with the chopped mint. Cover and set aside until ready to eat.

- Remove the steaks from the marinade, and grill over the barbecue for 2-3 minutes. The marinade can be made into a dressing by boiling rapidly for 2-3 minutes until it reduces and thickens. Cool, then pour over the salad.

WARM BARBECUE PUDDING

Ingredients
3 large ripe mangoes
2 bananas
2 kiwis
150ml/¼ pint dark rum
6 tablespoons soft brown sugar

Method
- Halve each mango either side of the stone, then peel away the skin. Remove any mango flesh left on the stone. Cut the mango into slices.
- Divide the mango between six pieces of foil. Peel and slice the bananas, dividing the slices between the mango. Repeat the process with the kiwi, and sprinkle the sugar over the fruit.
- Close up the foil, leaving an opening, then pour in the rum. Close the foil tightly. Place on the barbecue and cook for 5 minutes.
- Serve with ice-cream.

Vegetarian Dinner Party

For a seasonal change, why not try something a little different? Use the starter and dessert, and vary the main course between the two very different, but equally delicious, recipes in this section.

BLUE CHEESE AND CHIVE BALLS

Ingredients
225g/8oz blue cheese
225g/8oz cream cheese
2 tablespoons finely chopped chives and parsley, mixed
pinch of black pepper
rind and juice of ½ a lemon

Method
- Beat the cheeses together with the lemon rind and juice.

- Season with the pepper, then form into walnut-sized balls, and coat with the chives and parsley.

- Serve with a green salad and cherry tomatoes, with a dressing of 2 tablespoons of olive oil and 1 tablespoon of white wine vinegar shaken together in a jar.

ROAST PEPPERS WITH COURGETTE CURRY

Ingredients
2 large orange or red peppers
2 large yellow peppers
225g/8oz courgettes cut into rounds
2 tablespoons olive oil
50g/2oz mushrooms
1 teaspoon ground cumin
½ teaspoon chilli powder
1 teaspoon coriander
½ teaspoon turmeric
small tin chopped tomatoes
1 red chilli, de-seeded and chopped
50g/2oz pinenuts
110g/4oz white breadcrumbs
50g/2oz Parmesan cheese

Method
- To make the curry: heat the oil, add the spices, the garlic and the chilli, and fry for 1 minute.

- Add the courgettes, the tomatoes and the mushrooms. Cover and cook for 5-10 minutes.

- Cut the peppers lengthways, and remove the core and seeds. Place the cut side down on a baking tray, brush with a little oil and roast for 10 minutes at 200C/400F/Gas 6.

- Fill the peppers with the curry, scatter the pine nuts and cheese mixed with the breadcrumbs over the top.

- Cook in the oven for a further 10 minutes.

- Serve one half of a red pepper and one half of a yellow pepper per person.

- Garnish with salad leaves and herbs – basil, coriander or parsley – or serve with couscous.

CARROT AND HERB ROULADE

This delicious roulade will have even non-vegetarians clamouring for more – an excellent central dish for a dinner party, it pleases the eye and the tastebuds!

Ingredients
450g/1lb carrots
50g/2oz butter
4 large eggs
2 tablespoons chopped coriander, basil and parsley, mixed
salt and black pepper

The Filling
225g/8oz soft cream cheese
1 clove crushed garlic
1 tablespoon finely chopped mint
juice and rind of 1 lemon

Method
- Line a 30cm x 20cm/12" x 8" Swiss roll tin with parchment paper.

- Grate the carrots coarsely. In a large pan, melt the butter, stir in the carrots and cook gently over a low heat for about 5 minutes.

- Transfer to a large mixing bowl and allow to cool. Beat in the egg yolks and the herbs; season with salt and pepper.

- Whisk the egg whites until soft peaks appear, then fold into the carrot mixture.

- Pour the mixture into the prepared tin and spread evenly. Cook in a pre-heated oven at 200C/400F/Gas 6 for 10 minutes until risen and firm to the touch. Turn out onto a sheet of non-stick baking parchment, then cover with a damp cloth.

- Meanwhile, to prepare the cheese filling: mix the cheese, the lemon juice and rind, the crushed garlic and the mint together, and season to taste.

- Remove the cloth off the roulade, spread the cheese mixture over it and roll up as for a Swiss roll. Serve with salad or vegetables, and rice, pasta or potatoes.

BANANA AND MANGO MOUSSE

Serves 4

Ingredients
2 medium-sized ripe mangoes
3 bananas
juice of 1 lemon
75g/3oz caster sugar
4 tablespoons orange juice
150ml/¼ pint double cream
1 sachet vegetarian gelatine

Method
- Peel the mangoes and remove the flesh from the stone. Place into a food processor with the lemon juice, two of the bananas and the sugar. Blend until smooth.

- Bring the orange juice to the boil, sprinkle over the vegetarian gelatine and stir until dissolved. Mix into the fruit mixture.

- Whip the cream until it forms soft folds, and fold into the banana mixture.

- Pour into glass serving dishes and chill.

- Decorate with mango and banana slices, and a sprig of mint.

Summer Buffet

The delight of a buffet is that much of the cooking work can be done in advance. A loaded buffet table is also very pleasing to the eye! Here, I have suggested various possibilities – you could mix and match with your own favourites. The two desserts are just in case you really want to spoil your guests! As with a barbecue, serve as many salads as you like, and lots of fresh bread.

SALMON AND LEEK TART

Ingredients
The Pastry
225g/8oz plain flour
150g/5oz butter
pinch cayenne pepper
50g/2oz grated Parmesan or Cheddar cheese

The Filling
450g/1lb fresh salmon fillet, skinned
1 sliced orange
25g/1oz chopped parsley
225g/8oz finely chopped leeks
275ml/½ pint *crème fraîche*
150ml/¼ pint milk
4 large eggs
150ml/¼ pint white wine
freshly ground black pepper

Method
- To make the pastry: rub the butter into the flour until it resembles fine breadcrumbs.

- Mix in the cheese and the pepper and bind together with a little cold water. The pastry should be smooth and soft. Chill for 20 minutes before using.

- Roll out the pastry to fit a greased and lined deep flan tin 22cm/9" wide.

- Place the pastry over the rolling pin and gently place over the tin, gently pressing into the round. Trim the edges, pressing down with the palm of your hand. This prevents the pastry from shrinking.

- Cover with the baking parchment and add enough baking beans to cover the base. Cook for 15 minutes at 2000C/400F/Gas 6. Now remove the beans and paper and cook for a further 5 minutes.

- To prepare the filling: place the salmon in a large pan with the leeks, the orange slices and the white wine. Cover and gently simmer for 5 minutes.

- Drain the salmon, keeping the liquid, and flake into large pieces. Arrange in the pastry case with the leeks and the parsley.

- Whisk together the *crème fraîche*, the milk, the eggs and the salmon liquid, and season to taste. Then pour over the salmon, place the tin onto a baking sheet, and cook for about 30-40 minutes at 190C/375F/Gas 5 until the filling is golden and set.

- Serve hot or cold with a crisp green salad and orange segments, together with a glass of white wine.

- Note: individual tarts are quite useful to serve, or use an oblong fluted tin and then cut into slices.

SUMMER CURRIED CHICKEN WITH MELON AND TOMATO SALAD

Ingredients
4 cooked chicken breasts
225g/8oz finely chopped onion
1 garlic clove
½ teaspoon chilli powder
1 teaspoon ground coriander and cumin
4 tablespoons mango chutney
rind and juice of 1 lemon
150ml/¼ pint natural yogurt
275ml/½ pint mayonnaise
150ml/¼ pint double cream
half a honeydew melon
450g/1lb tomatoes, cut into slices, or cherry tomatoes
1 tablespoon olive oil
chilli or cayenne pepper to garnish with parsley

Method
- Heat the oil in a frying pan. Cook the onions, the garlic and the spices for about 5 minutes.

- Add the lemon rind and juice, and the mango chutney, and mix well. Leave the mixture to cool, then mix in the yogurt, the mayonnaise and the cream.

- Cut the chicken breasts into large strips and mix into the sauce. Chill until required.

- Cut the melon in half, remove the seeds, cut into wedges and remove the skin, then cut into chunks, or use a melon baller to make balls.

- To serve: arrange the melon and tomato on a serving plate, top with some chicken curry, and garnish with cayenne pepper and parsley – simply delicious!

SPICY VEGETABLES WITH COUSCOUS

Serves 4

I am not a vegetarian myself, but spicy foods certainly appeal to me. You could use any vegetables of your choice and include cheese if you wish.

Ingredients

2 red onions, peeled and cut into wedges
225g/8oz carrots, peeled and thinly sliced
225g/8oz cauliflower florets
2 cloves garlic
1 teaspoon ground cumin
1 teaspoon ground turmeric
1 teaspoon cinnamon
225g/8oz couscous
3 tablespoons olive oil
200g/7oz can butter beans, strained
400ml/14 fl oz vegetable stock for the couscous
275ml/½ pint vegetable stock
275ml/½ pint tomato juice
2 tablespoons chopped fresh parsley

Method

- Place the couscous in a heatproof bowl with a pinch of salt and 1 tablespoon olive oil. Then pour over the vegetable stock. Cover and leave to stand for 5 minutes until the grains are swollen and all the liquid absorbed.

- Heat the remaining oil in a large pan, add the onions and the carrots, then cook for 4-5 minutes until the onions are soft.

- Now add the spices, the garlic, the cauliflower and the butter beans, the stock and the tomato juice. Bring to the boil and cook for 5 minutes.

- Fluff up the couscous, add the parsley, and place into a shallow serving bowl.

- Serve the vegetables on top.

- Garnish with more parsley and coriander.

- Note: vegetarian cheese could be added to the couscous.

GARLIC POTATO SALAD

Ingredients
700g/1½ lbs cooked new or old potatoes
175ml/6fl oz mayonnaise
juice of 1 lemon
2 cloves of garlic, crushed
1 finely chopped onion
1 tablespoon chopped chives
1 tablespoon chopped parsley
salt and pepper to taste

Method
- Cut the potatoes into bite-size pieces, and place in a bowl. Add the chopped onion, the lemon juice, the garlic, the chives and the parsley.

- Mix in the mayonnaise and season to taste.

- Cover and refrigerate for 1-2 hours to obtain the full flavour.

SUMMER PUDDINGS WITH RASPBERRY AND BLACKCURRANT SAUCE

This is a very popular summer dessert. Picking your own fruits from our well-organised fruit farms is a real pleasure. Raspberries, strawberries, red-currants and blackcurrants are my favourites, and these puddings can be frozen for up to 3-4 months.

You will also need 4 small basins or moulds, each with 225ml/8oz capacity.

Ingredients
700g/1½ lbs mixed strawberries,
    raspberries and blackcurrants
50g/2oz caster sugar
grated rind and juice of 1 lemon
55ml/2 fl oz redcurrant juice
16 medium-thick slices of white bread

The Sauce
225g/8oz blackcurrants
225g/8oz raspberries
175g/6oz caster sugar

Method
- Place the prepared fruit into a heavy-based pan with the sugar, the lemon rind and juice. Gently bring it to the boil, then remove from the heat.

- Strain the fruit, reserve all the juice and leave to cool.

- Cut the crusts off the bread, cut 4 rounds to the size of your mould and dip into the juice. Place in the base of the mould. Cut 8 slices of bread into rectangles to fit the mould, dip into fruit juice, then line the sides of each mould.

- Divide the fruit between each mould. Cut the remaining bread into 4 circles the size of the mould, dip into fruit juice and cover the top. Cover tightly with clingfilm and chill overnight.

- To make the sauce: place the fruit and sugar into a heavy-based saucepan and gently heat until the sugar has melted. Remove from the heat. Place into a food processor for 3-4 seconds, then sieve to remove all the seeds.

- To serve the pudding: turn the moulds upside down to remove the puddings, pour a little sauce and a spoonful of *crème fraîche* or double cream over them.

RHUBARB AND ORANGE
MERINGUE FLAN

Serves 6-8

*Rhubarb and orange marry well together in flavour with a hint of ginger.
Rhubarb is always best in season. This makes a lovely summer pudding.*

Ingredients
The Pastry
23cm/9" quiche or flan tin
110g/4oz soft butter
110g/4oz caster sugar
3 large egg yolks
175g/6oz strong plain flour
25g/1oz ground almonds

The Meringue
3 egg whites
175g/6oz caster sugar

The Filling
700g/1½ lbs rhubarb
3 oranges
110g/4oz caster sugar
3 egg yolks
2 level tablespoons cornflour
1 teaspoon ground ginger

Method
- To make the pastry: cream the butter and sugar together, then beat in the eggs. Fold in the flour and ground almonds. Turn onto a floured surface and knead lightly. Wrap in clingfilm and chill for 30 minutes.

- Roll out the pastry on to a floured work surface and line the tin with grease-proof paper. Prick the pastry base with a fork, line with greaseproof paper and baking beans.

- Cook for 15-20 minutes at 180C/350F/Gas 4, then remove the beans and paper from the pastry and return to the oven for 5 minutes to dry.

- To make the filling: wipe the rhubarb and cut into small chunks. Grate the orange rind and add to the rhubarb.

- With a sharp knife, remove the pith from the orange, then remove the orange segments and add to the rhubarb. Squeeze all the juice from the orange core into the rhubarb.

- Place the rhubarb in a saucepan with the sugar and the ginger, bring to the boil, then simmer for 2-3 minutes until the rhubarb is cooked.

- Thicken with blended cornflour and cook until the mixture is clear. Beat in the egg yolks, then pour the mixture into the cooked pastry case.

- To make the meringue: place the egg whites into a large, clean bowl, and whisk until stiff.

- Gradually beat in the sugar until the meringue becomes stiff and glossy. Spoon the meringue over the rhubarb.

- Cook for 15-20 minutes at 180C/350F/Gas 4 until golden brown. Slide the flan onto a plate and serve with double cream.

- Note: summer fruits could also be used instead of the egg yolks for the filling.

Summer Celebration

This is a wonderful menu for a family celebration. Whether it's a christening, an engagement, a birthday, an anniversary, or just a reason to get the family together, the luxury of this menu will certainly add to the festivities!

PAN GRILLED SCALLOPS
WITH PEPPER SAUCE
Serves 4

Ingredients
12 scallops
50g/2oz unsalted butter
4 slices brown or white bread
110g/4oz bag of mixed baby leaf salad
2 tablespoons olive oil

The Sauce
3 red peppers
1 glass white wine
salt and pepper
1 bunch of chives
1 tablespoon olive oil
4 lemon slices
juice of 1 lemon

Method

- To prepare the scallops: wash in plenty of cold water, hold the scallop flat shell uppermost and slide the blade of a filleting knife between the shells, keeping the blade flat against the top shell. Feel for the ligament that joins the shell to the muscle meat of the scallop and cut through.

- Lift the top shell and pull out the black stomach sac and the frilly 'skirt'. Cut the scallop meat away from the shell. Pull off and discard the small white ligament that is attached to the side of the scallop meat.

- To make the sauce: cut the peppers in half and remove the seeds. Place on a baking tray and brush with olive oil. Place under a hot grill until the skin turns black. Remove the skin, and place the pepper flesh in a blender with the wine, the olive oil, the seasoning and the lemon juice.

- Heat a grill pan, melt the butter until frothy, and quickly fry the scallops for 30 seconds on each side.

- To make the croûtons: cut a large circle out of each slice of bread and quickly fry in a little oil and butter until crisp.

- Arrange the croûtons on a serving plate. Place 3 scallops on each croûton, arrange the salad leaves around them, then drizzle the pepper sauce over the salad, with a slice of lemon. Scatter the chives over the plate.

ROASTED BONED CHICKEN WITH DUCK BREASTS AND STUFFING

Ingredients
1 chicken about 3.6kg/8lbs in weight
4 duck breasts, skin removed

The Stuffing
450g/1lb pork sausagemeat
3 small onions, finely chopped
225g/8oz cooked chestnuts
350g/12oz white breadcrumbs
good bunch chopped parsley
1 teaspoon dried thyme and sage
225g/8oz fresh apricots cut in quarters, stones removed
110g/4oz butter
salt and pepper

The Gravy
570ml/1 pint of chicken stock
2 tablespoons cranberry sauce
1 tablespoon cornflour

Method
- To bone the chicken: run a sharp knife down the backbone of the chicken and remove all the flesh from one side, then the other side, being careful not to cut the skin. Remove the leg joints and wing joints from the carcass.

- Leaving the wing bones on, remove the top bone from the leg joint.

- To make the stuffing: fry the onion in hot butter for 3-4 minutes. Add the sausagemeat, the breadcrumbs, the apricots, the herbs, the chestnuts and the seasoning. Mix thoroughly.

- Place the duck breasts along the middle of the chicken carcass.

- Then place the stuffing down the centre, filling the leg with stuffing to mould it and keep its shape.

- Using a trussing needle and strong string, sew the chicken up, going from one side to the other. When you come to the legs, sew them up to the body.

- Turn the chicken over, breast side up, and plump up the chicken by shaping the wings under the body. Use a skewer to secure the legs to the body.

- Place the chicken in a roasting tin with a little water, sprinkle with salt, and rub the skin with some butter.

- Roast the chicken for about 1½ hours at 200C/400F/Gas 6.

- When the chicken is cooked, place on a large serving dish.

- Pour away any excess fat from the roasting tin, then pour in the gravy ingredients and whisk well. Make sure you get all the sediment from the tin, bring to the boil, and season to taste.

- Serve with vegetables of your choice.

COX'S APPLE PUDDING WITH LEMON AND REAL CUSTARD

Ingredients
Scone dough
225g/8oz self-raising flour
75g/3oz butter
pinch of nutmeg
pinch of cinnamon
rind of 1 lemon
150ml/¼ pint milk (you may not need it all)
1 egg yolk
1 egg white
1 tablespoon Demerara sugat

The Filling
700g/1½ lbs Cox's apples, cored, peeled and sliced
50g/2oz butter
50g/2oz Demerara sugar
50g/3 tablespoons lemon marmalade
50g/2oz ground almonds

The Custard
275ml/½ pint double cream
275ml/½ pint milk
5 egg yolks
1 vanilla pod
50g/2oz caster sugar
2 teaspoons cornflour

Method
- To make the dough: rub the butter into the flour to resemble fine bread-crumbs, then mix in the spices and the lemon rind. Add the milk gradually to make a soft, but firm dough. Leave to rest while making the filling.

- To make the filling: heat the butter and the sugar in a large frying pan, stir in the sliced apples, and cook for 2-3 minutes until the apples have been glazed all over.

- Mix the marmalade in with the apples. Leave to cool slightly.

- On a floured surface, roll out the dough to roughly 35cm/14 inches. Place the pastry on a greased baking tray. Paint the base of the dough with the egg yolk to prevent it becoming soggy. Then sprinkle with the ground almonds.

- Spoon the apple mixture into the centre, then turn in the dough edges. This should have a rugged look. Brush with egg white and sprinkle with the Demerara sugar.

- Cook on the middle shelf of a hot oven at 200C/400F/Gas 6 for 15-20 minutes until golden brown. Remove from the oven and serve hot with real custard.

- To make the custard: pour the cream and the milk into a heavy-based saucepan with the vanilla pod and slowly bring to the boil. Leave for 10 minutes for the vanilla to infuse into the milk.

- Whisk together the yolks, the sugar and the cornflour, then pour in the milk. Pour back into the saucepan, and heat through gently, whisking all the time until the custard has thickened.

- Tip: other fruit may be used, but use in season, e.g. rhubarb, gooseberries, cherries, apricots, blackcurrants, plums, or combine blackberries and apples.

AUTUMN

Crisp, clear mornings and 'mists and mellow fruitfulness' make autumn a lovely bridge between summer and winter. Harvest time brings excellent cooking opportunities, and I hope you will enjoy the menus for this particular season.

MENUS

Autumn Tasters

Crab and Orange Mousse
Lamb Hotpot
Tropical Fruit Crumble

Quick and Easy

Papaya and Prawn Salad
Mustard and Peppered Welsh Beef with Pasta Shells
Nice and Easy Puddings
Peppered Welsh Beef and Mustard with Pasta Shells

Vegetarian Dinner

Stuffed Marrow Rings
Deep Vegetarian Savoury Tart
Orange Sorbet

Autumn Entertaining

Potato and Parsley Soup
Soda Bread
Braised Beef in Guinness
Chocolate Fudge Pudding

Autumn Tasters

CRAB AND ORANGE MOUSSE

Crab and orange flavour work well together; this recipe is ideal as a starter, or a light lunch. If you do not like crab, try tinned or freshly cooked salmon.

Ingredients
450g/1lb shredded crab; tinned, fresh or frozen
350g/12oz cream cheese
2 tablespoons seafood dressing
juice and rind of ½ an orange
1 teaspoon mustard
2 tablespoons chopped chives
salt and pepper to taste
1 sachet gelatine

Method
- Place all the ingredients (except the chives and the gelatine) into a food processor and blend until smooth.
- Melt the gelatine in 3 tablespoons of boiling water and stir until dissolved and smooth, then pour into the crab mixture. Mix well, and stir in the chopped chives.
- Divide between six ramekin dishes, place into the fridge until set for 1-2 hours. This can be done the day before.
- To serve: turn the mousses out on to a serving plate, and garnish with a little side salad.

LAMB HOTPOT

Ingredients
450g/1lb leg of lamb, cut into 5cm/2" pieces
225g /8oz shallots
1 crushed clove of garlic
225g/8oz button mushrooms
1 large cooking apple, peeled, cored and chopped
large bunch of mint
400g/14oz tin chopped tomatoes
275ml/½ pint wine
275ml/½ pint apple juice
pepper and salt
1 tablespoon olive oil

The Dumplings
110g/4oz self-raising flour
50g/2oz shredded suet
1 tablespoon chopped parsley
salt and pepper
a little water to bind

Method
- Heat the oil in a large pan, toss in the lamb and the shallots and fry until brown to seal in the lovely juices.

- Add the garlic, the mushrooms, the apple, the tomato, the wine and the apple juice. Bring to the boil, cover and simmer for 15 minutes.

- In the meantime make the dumplings. Place the flour in a bowl with the suet and the parsley and bind together with very little water. The dough must be quite firm. Then divide into 8 dumplings

- Now add the dumplings to the lamb, cover and cook for a further 15 minutes.

- Season the hotpot to taste. If you think the sauce needs a little thickening, add some blended cornflour. Finally, add the chopped mint and serve with vegetables.

TROPICAL FRUIT CRUMBLE

Serves 4-6

Today, crumble is made in many ways, using muesli, oats, crunchy oat cereal, Amaretti biscuits and nuts, making crumble more of a classy and healthy pudding. It can be served with crème fraîche, yogurt, cream or custard. Any fruit can be used – I recommend using fruit in season.

Ingredients

1 medium pineapple	1 ripe mango
2 bananas	2 tablespoons Malibu liqueur
2 papays	1 teaspoon cinnamon
4 kiwi fruits	1 teaspoon nutmeg
1 Galia melon	2 tablespoons Demerara sugar
1 Charentais melon	juice and rind of 1 lime

The Topping
225g/8oz oat cereal with raisins, honey, and flaked almonds
110g/4oz butter

Method
- Prepare the fruit. Cut the skin off the pineapple and cut into small pieces. Cut the papaya in half, remove the seeds and skin and cut into small chunks.
- Cut the melons in half, remove the seeds and, using a melon baller, remove the flesh from the skin.
- Cut the flesh from the mango stone, then remove from the skin and cut into chunks.
- Now mix together all the fruit with the lime juice and rind, the spices and the Malibu.
- To make the topping: melt the butter and stir into the crunchy oat cereal.
- You can make the crumble in individual dishes or in a large dish, placing a little topping on the bottom, adding a layer of fruit, then another layer of topping.
- Sprinkle with a little Demerara sugar and bake for 15 minutes at 180C/350F/ Gas 4.
- Serve with *crème fraîche* or mango sauce (see over) and garnish with mint.

Alternative Topping 1
225g/8oz Amaretti biscuits
50g/2oz butter
1 tablespoon honey

Method
- Crush the biscuits lightly.

- Melt the butter and honey, toss in the lightly crushed biscuits.

- Place on top of the fruit and cook as on page 64.

Alternative Topping 2
175g/6oz self-raising flour
50g/2oz porridge oats
50g/2oz butter
50g/2oz Demerara sugar

Method
- Rub the butter into the flour until it resembles fine breadcrumbs. Mix in the oats and sugar.

- Place on top of the fruit and cook as above.

MANGO SAUCE

Ingredients
1 mango, peeled and flesh removed from the stone
275ml/½ pint *crème fraîche*
1 tablespoon Malibu liqueur

Method
- Pulp the mango flesh by hand or in a processor.

- Mix all the ingredients together well and serve with the crumble.

Quick and Easy

PAPAYA AND PRAWN SALAD

This is a light and fresh starter to a meal, ready to serve in about 10 minutes. King prawns are available at most fishmongers, fresh or frozen.

Ingredients
2-3 ripe papayas
350g/12oz cooked prawns
2 tablespoons clear honey
salt and pepper
2 small red chillies
2 tablespoons white wine vinegar
2 tablespoons parsley
juice of 2 limes (3 to 4 tablespoons)
150ml/5 fl oz olive oil
4-6 king prawns, cooked

Method
- Chop the chillies, discarding the seeds. Place in a blender with the vinegar, the lime juice, the honey, the olive oil and the parsley. Blend until smooth.
- Toss the prawns in the dressing. Cut the papaya in half, remove the seeds and peel.
- Thinly slice the fruit and arrange on plates.
- Spoon the prawn mixture over the papaya, serve immediately, or keep chilled until required.
- Top with the king prawns in their shells.

PEPPERED WELSH BEEF AND MUSTARD WITH PASTA SHELLS

This is a great dish to cook if you are suddenly faced with unexpected guests. Prepared and cooked in half an hour, Welsh beef is a great choice of meat.

Ingredients

350g/12oz rump steak cut into thick strips
225g/8oz mushrooms, sliced
ground black pepper
1 tablespoon ground mustard seeds
4 tablespoons brandy
110g/4oz Welsh butter
2 tablespoons wholegrain mustard
2 tablespoon chopped parsley
1 teaspoon anchovy essence
bunch spring onions, finely sliced
200ml/7fl oz *crème fraîche*
350g/12oz cooked pasta shells
chopped chives

Method

- Toss the steaks in the black pepper and mustard seeds.

- Heat 75g/3oz of the butter in a heavy-based frying pan until hot. Cook the beef strips in batches for 2-3 minutes at a time.

- Remove the beef from the pan into a bowl or plate, then heat the remaining butter and cook the mushrooms and spring onions for 1 minute.

- Pour in the brandy and the *crème fraîche* and bring to the boil. Simmer for 1-2 minutes.

- Stir in the anchovy essence, the mustard and the parsley. Return the beef to the sauce and bring to the boil.

- Serve with the cooked pasta shells.

- Garnish with the chives.

NICE AND EASY PUDDINGS

Ingredients
450g/1lb strawberries, hulled
275 ml/½ pint double cream
225g/8oz cream cheese
rind of 1 orange
4 tablespoons clear honey
4 tablespoons brandy
Amaretti biscuits
mint leaves

Method
- Place two biscuits each into four tall glass dessert dishes. Spoon over a little brandy.
- Reserve four strawberries, then slice the remaining strawberries, and place into the glasses. Spoon a little more brandy over the strawberries.
- Whip the double cream to a soft consistency.
- Fold into the cream cheese, orange rind and honey.
- Spoon the cheese mixture over the strawberries, decorate with two Amaretti biscuits, and a strawberry (cut into a fan shape) with a mint leaf.

Vegetarian Dinner

STUFFED MARROW RINGS

Marrow is in season from July to October, and young home-grown marrows are the best. Stuffed baked marrow makes a lovely starter or supper, served with a rich, creamy cheese sauce.

Ingredients
1 marrow, about 1.35kg/3lbs
3 small leeks
1 red apple, cored
1 green apple, cored
225g/8oz short back bacon
½ teaspoon nutmeg
½ teaspoon paprika
1 clove crushed garlic
50g/2oz butter
1 tablespoon olive oil
2 tablespoons cider vinegar
1 tablespoon Demerara sugar
salt and pepper
110g/4oz white breadcrumbs

The Cheese Sauce
275ml/½ pint double cream
110g/4oz Welsh Cheddar cheese
pinch of paprika
4 finely chopped spring onions

Method
- Peel the marrow, then cut into 7.5cm/3" depth rings. Remove the pith and seeds from the inside of the rings. Place the marrow rings on a greased baking tray.

- To prepare the filling: wash and chop the leeks finely, chop the apples finely. Cut the bacon into small pieces.

- In a large frying pan, melt a little butter, the oil and the Demerara sugar. Fry the prepared fruit and vegetables, the bacon and the garlic. These will caramelise slightly after 2-3 minutes.

- To the mixture, add the spices and the vinegar, and cook for a further 2-3 minutes.

- Spoon the mixture into the marrow rings. Sprinkle over some breadcrumbs, place a knob of butter on each. Cover with foil and bake for 20 minutes at 180C/350F/Gas 4.

- To make the sauce: pour the cream into a non-stick pan with the spring onions and cheese. Gently bring to the boil, allowing the cheese to melt. Season with a little salt and paprika.

- Serve the marrow with the cheese sauce, garnished with chopped parsley and grilled tomatoes.

DEEP VEGETARIAN SAVOURY TART

This is an ideal recipe for a special vegetarian dinner party, using filo pastry for the base.

Ingredients
225g/8oz mushrooms, sliced
2 courgettes, sliced
2 tablespoons tomato purée
1 tablespoon chopped oregano leaves
1 onion, sliced
450g/1lb can artichoke hearts, drained and chopped
225g/8oz vegetarian Cheddar cheese, grated
110g/4oz chopped walnuts
2 large tomatoes
6 large sheets of filo pastry
50g/2oz melted butter
black pitted olives

You will need a 20cm/8" or 23cm/9" spring-form flan tin, lined with baking parchment.

Method
- Line the flan tin with filo pastry, brushing between all 6 layers with the butter. Allow the pastry to overlap the tin slightly.

- Heat a little oil in a large saucepan, and gently cook the mushrooms, the courgettes and the onion for 2-3 minutes.

- Add the tomato purée, the oregano, the chopped artichokes and the walnuts. Mix well.

- Spoon the mixture into the lined flan tin, sprinkle over the grated cheese, arrange slices of tomato on top and scatter some black pitted olives over them. Cover the top with the pastry.

- Cook for 30 minutes until golden brown, at 180C/350F/Gas 4.

- Serve with green vegetables and potatoes in your favourite style.

ORANGE SORBET

Ingredients
finely grated rind and juice of 3 oranges
finely grated rind and juice of 1 lemon
175g/6oz granulated sugar
570 ml/1 pint water
1 egg white

Method
- Place the orange and lemon rinds in a large saucepan with sugar and water.
- Dissolve the sugar slowly, then bring to the boil and boil for 10 minutes.
- Remove the saucepan from the heat and allow the syrup to cool completely.
- Add the strained fruit juices and pour into a suitable container. Cover and place in the freezer or ice-making part of the refrigerator, until the mixture is thick and slushy.
- Beat the egg white and fold it into the fruit mixture. Return the mixture to the freezer and freeze until stiff.
- Remove the sorbet from the freezer 10 minutes before serving.
- Variations: for Lemon Sorbet, use the rind of 2 lemons and the juice of 3 lemons.
- For Raspberry or Strawberry Sorbet: add 425ml/¾ pint fruit purée, and the juice of ½ lemon to 570ml/1 pint of syrup.

POTATO AND PARSLEY SOUP

Soups are a favourite of mine. Most people have potatoes and onions in the house, even if your store cupboard is rather empty! So do try this easy, delicious soup.

Ingredients
450g/1lb peeled and diced old potatoes
50g/2oz butter
225g/8oz sliced onions
1 teaspoon sea salt
freshly ground black pepper
1 teaspoon ground nutmeg
1.1l/1½ pints chicken or vegetable stock
6-8 parsley stalks
130ml/4fl oz creamy milk
chopped parsley to garnish

Method
- Melt the butter in a heavy saucepan, add the potatoes and onion, gently sauté for 2-3 minutes. Sprinkle with salt, ground pepper and nutmeg.
- Add the parsley stalks and stock. Cook covered until the vegetables are cooked (about 15 minutes).
- Remove the stalks and purée the soup in a blender.
- Season to taste, stir in the milk and parsley.
- Serve with soda bread (see recipe on p.74).

SODA BREAD

You can make a variety of soda bread adding olives, sun-dried tomatoes or caramelised onions to the mixture.

Ingredients
450g/1lb strong plain flour
1 teaspoon salt
1 teaspoon bicarbonate of soda
425ml/15 fl oz buttermilk or sour milk

Method
- Place all the dry ingredients into a bowl. Mix with the milk to form a soft dough, which is not too wet or too sticky. When it all comes together turn out onto a floured board and knead lightly.

- Pat the dough into a circle, then cut a cross on top with a knife. Bake for about 15 minutes at 200C/400F/Gas 6.

- Tap the bottom of the bread to check whether it is cooked. If it is ready, it will sound hollow.

BRAISED BEEF IN GUINNESS

Serves 4

Ingredients
900g/2lbs good quality braising steak, cut into large chunks
225g/8oz onions, finely sliced
225g/8oz carrots, diced
2 cloves garlic
275ml/½ pint Guinness
275ml/½ pint beef stock
1 teaspoon salt
black pepper
2 teaspoons mustard
225g/8oz bacon, cut into small pieces
2 tablespoons olive oil
50g/2oz butter
bayleaf, parsley, thyme, and sage sprigs
50g/2oz seasoned flour

The Dumplings
225g/8oz self-raising flour
110g/4oz shredded suet
2 teaspoons mixed dried herbs
salt and pepper
a little water to bind together

Method
- Toss the beef in the seasoned flour.
- Heat the oil and butter in a large saucepan. Fry the bacon and the beef until browned, add the onion and the carrots, then fry for a further 2 minutes.
- Add the garlic and the mustard, and stir in the stock and the Guinness. Gently bring to the boil, and add the seasoning and the herbs. Cover and simmer for about 1 hour, or cook in the oven, until the meat is tender.
- To make the dumplings: mix together the flour, the suet, the herbs and the seasoning with enough water to make a soft dough. Divide into eight small balls, and add them to the saucepan. Simmer for about 15 minutes, covered.
- Season to taste and sprinkle over plenty of freshly chopped parsley.

CHOCOLATE FUDGE PUDDINGS

Serves 6

Chocolate puddings are most people's favourite dessert. These are really wicked and rich, with a melting texture. They should be moist in the centre, so do not overcook. They are also delicious eaten cold.

Ingredients
140g/5 oz good quality chocolate, minimum 70% cocoa solids
140g/5 oz butter
1 teaspoon pure vanilla
150ml/¼ pint warm water
110g/4 oz caster sugar
4 eggs
25g/1 oz self-raising flour

Method
- Cut the chocolate into pieces and place in a bowl with the butter. Place the bowl over a pan of warm water and melt gently.

- Remove from the heat, add the vanilla, the warm water and the caster sugar. Stir until the mixture is smooth.

- Separate the eggs, whisk the yolks into the chocolate, then sieve the flour and fold in.

- Whisk the egg whites in a clean bowl until it forms soft peaks. Then gently fold into the chocolate mixture.

- Divide between six ramekin dishes, then place onto a baking tray in a little water, and bake for about 15 minutes at 180C/350F/Gas 4.

- The puddings should be firm on top but still soft and fudgy underneath.

- Serve hot or cold with whipped cream.

WINTER

*I know it's cold, wet and sometimes unpleasant, but winter brings
many good things, especially to the table. Warming soups with
crusty bread, lovely root vegetables and, best of all, Christmas fare!
There is a special section on breads at the end of these menus,
so that you can vary your baking over the winter, which,
don't forget, is followed by spring . . .*

MENUS

Winter Warmers

Winter Vegetable Soup
Baked Cod with Baked Potatoes and Carmarthen Ham
Apple and Pear Soufflé Omelette

Alternative Christmas Lunch

Fillets of Hake with Bacon and Buttery Sauce
Stuffed Roast Sirloin of Welsh Black Beef
Vegetable Accompaniments
Bubble and Squeak Cakes with Onion Marmalade
Ginger Cake
Luxury Mincemeat Almond Slices

Vegetarian Winter Dinner

Spicy Lentil Soup
Chestnut, Leek and Cranberry Ring
Warm Pear Pudding with Coconut Custard

Bread Selection

Basic Brown and White Bread
Malted Granary Bread
Ciabatta
Cornbread
Muesli Bread

WINTER VEGETABLE SOUP   **Serves 6**

To get the best flavour out of any vegetables, they should be used in season. There are so many healthy and nutritious vegetables available in winter: carrots; swedes; cabbage; cauliflower; broccoli; parsnips; onions; leeks and potatoes, to name a few favourites. This soup is just delicious, with some spices added to the natural flavour of the vegetables.

Ingredients

3 carrots
1 small swede
1 onion
2 parsnips
2 leeks
1 small celeriac
1 small cabbage
salt and pepper

1.4l-1.7l/2½-3 pints of vegetable stock or water
1 small red chilli, de-seeded and chopped
½ teaspoon nutmeg
½ teaspoon cinnamon
2 cloves garlic, crushed
bunch of parsley

Method

- Clean and chop all the vegetables (except the cabbage and the leeks) into bite-size pieces.

- Wash and shred the cabbage and the leeks.

- Place the carrots, the swede, the onion, the parsnips and the celeriac in a large saucepan. Add the chilli, the spices and the garlic.

- Pour in the stock and add salt and pepper. Bring to the boil, cover and simmer for 30 minutes.

- Add the shredded cabbage and leeks to the soup. Cover and cook for 5 minutes.

- If the soup is too thick, add a little more stock.

- Season to taste, and stir in the fresh chopped parsley.

- Serve in a bowl, topped with grated Parmesan cheese, and bread.

BAKED COD WITH BAKED POTATOES AND CARMARTHEN HAM

We should eat fish three or four times a week as it is so nutritious and tasty, as well as being easy to prepare. Why not try this freshly baked cod, with a parsley herb crust, served with sliced potatoes and Carmarthen ham? You can vary the dish by using other fish, such as hake, haddock or monkfish.

Ingredients

4 portions of skinless cod
  (175g/6oz each)
225g/8oz white breadcrumbs
1 tablespoon chopped parsley
a few sprigs fresh thyme
1 tablespoon chopped chives
50g/2oz melted butter
salt and pepper
3 lemons
1 garlic bulb
2-3 tablespoons olive oil

Baked Potatoes with Carmarthen Ham

700g/1½ lbs potatoes, scrubbed and
  thinly sliced
2 large onions, thinly sliced
175g/6oz pack of Carmarthen ham
salt and pepper
a little olive oil
sage leaves and thyme

Method

- Place the fish in an ovenproof gratin dish, then cut the lemons into slices, and cut the garlic bulb in half. Place the cloves around the fish.

- To make the herb crust: mix together the breadcrumbs, the herbs and the butter. Divide the breadcrumbs between the fish. Drizzle over a little oil, and bake at 200C/400F/Gas 6 for 20-30 minutes.

- To prepare the potatoes: arrange a layer of potato slices in a greased ovenproof gratin dish. Cover with a layer of onions, some sage leaves, and thyme, salt and pepper, then a layer of Carmarthen ham.

- Repeat the layer sequence once more, ending with a layer of potatoes. Season with salt and pepper, drizzle over a little oil and bake in the oven for 20-30 minutes at the same temperature as the fish.

- Serve with a fresh crisp green salad, or roasted peppers.

APPLE AND PEAR SOUFFLÉ OMELETTE

Sometimes we look for a quick but tasty pudding recipe. This omelette takes only 20 minutes to prepare and cook – an excellent solution to a sweet crisis!

Ingredients
450g/1 lb eating apples
450g/1 lb Conference pears
110g/4 oz unsalted butter
75g/3 oz caster sugar
rind and juice of 2 lemons
75g/3 oz white breadcrumbs
4 eggs, separated
150ml/¼ pint double cream

Method
- Peel and core the apples and pears, then cut into 2.5cm/1" chunks.

- Heat the butter and lemon rind slowly in a 25cm/10" non-stick frying pan. Stir the apples and pears into the melted butter and cook for 2-3 minutes over a low heat.

- Add the sugar and the lemon juice, mixing well until the sugar has melted. Mix in the breadcrumbs to absorb all the juices.

- Mix the egg yolks and cream together, whisk the egg whites to form soft peaks, and fold into the egg yolks.

- Pour the egg mixture over the fruit in the pan, stir it gently, then cook in the oven at 180C/350F/Gas 4 for 15 minutes until the egg mixture is golden brown and set, **or** complete cooking on your hob for 3-4 minutes, and then pop under the grill to brown.

- To serve: slide onto a plate, dust with icing sugar, cut into 4 portions with a spoonful of double cream and a sprig of mint – delicious!

Papaya and Prawn Salad: Autumn (p. 66).

Peppered Welsh Beef and Mustard with Pasta Shells: Autumn (p. 67).

Chocolate Fudge Puddings: Autumn (p. 76).

Fillets of Hake with Bacon in Buttery Sauce: Winter (p. 81).

Bubble and Squeak Cakes with Onion Marmalade: Winter (p. 85).

Chestnut, Leek and Cranberry Ring: Winter (p. 89).

Warm Pear Pudding: Winter (p. 91).

A Selection of Bread: Winter (pp. 93-100).

Alternative Christmas Lunch

FILLETS OF HAKE WITH BACON AND BUTTERY SAUCE

This simple recipe is ideal as a starter or a main course. When buying fish, ensure that it is bright, and smells fresh.

Ingredients
700g-900g/1½-2 lbs hake fillet
8 slices of thin smoked bacon
50g/2 oz seasoned plain flour
3 tablespoons sunflower oil
pepper and salt

The Sauce
2 tablespoons finely chopped
   parsley, chives and tarragon, mixed
50g/2oz unsalted butter
1 shallot, finely sliced
175ml/6 fl oz champagne or white
   wine
110ml/4 fl oz fish stock
110ml/4 fl oz double cream
juice of 1 lemon

Method
- Toss the hake fillets in the seasoned flour. Heat the oil in a grill pan, then fry the hake skin side down first until the skin is crisp.

- Turn over and cook for a further 1-2 minutes. Remove from the pan and keep warm.

- To the pan, add the shallot, the champagne, the lemon juice, the stock and the cream. Bring to the boil and reduce to three quarters. Mix in the butter. Season to taste, then mix in the herbs.

- Grill the bacon until crisp.

- Arrange the hake fillets on a serving plate with the bacon, pour the sauce around, garnish with lemon slices.

- Cod, haddock, trout, sea bass, or even plaice could be used for this recipe.

STUFFED ROAST SIRLOIN
OF WELSH BLACK BEEF

Serves 12

This makes a stunning centrepiece for a Christmas table if you're looking for an alternative to turkey. Serve with your favourite vegetables.

Ingredients
3.1kg/7lbs cut sirloin beef
450g/1lb cooked tinned chestnuts
225g/8oz sausagemeat
110g/4oz white breadcrumbs
1 teaspoon mixed herbs
2 tablespoons chopped parsley
juice and rind of 1 orange
1 onion, finely chopped
110g/4oz chopped mushrooms
25g/1oz sea salt
half a bottle of red wine

Yorkshire Pudding
110g/4oz strong plain flour
2 eggs
275ml/½ pint milk
1 tablespoon cold water
pinch salt

The Gravy
plain flour
150ml/5 fl oz red wine
570ml/1 pint vegetable stock
2 tablespoons redcurrant jelly

Method
- Cook the onion and the mushrooms in a little hot oil.

- In a large bowl, mix together the sausagemeat, the herbs, the chestnuts, the parsley, the breadcrumbs, the orange juice and rind and a little salt and pepper. Add the cooked onion and mushroom and make sure they are thoroughly mixed.

- Lay the beef flat on a board, place the stuffing down the centre and roll, tying with string at intervals.

- Place the beef in a roasting tin. Rub with salt – this will give the meat a lovely crunchy texture. Pour half a bottle of red wine into the tin.

- Roast in the oven for about 1½-2 hours, depending on how well cooked or rare you like the meat, at 200C/400F/Gas 6. When cooked, remove from the tin on to a carving plate and leave to rest.

- To make the gravy: spoon away any excess fat from the roasting tin. Sprinkle about 1-2 tablespoons of plain flour into the tin and stir.

- Pour in the vegetable stock and the wine with two tablespoons of redcurrant jelly. Bring to the boil and simmer for 3-4 minutes.

- Make sure you have stirred the gravy well, combining all the flavours from the bottom of the roasting tin.

- Season to taste.

- To make the Yorkshire pudding: place the flour into a bowl with the salt.

- Whisk in the eggs and milk, until you have a smooth batter. Stir in some iced water. Leave to stand for half an hour before cooking.

- Pour a little oil into a 30cm/12" patty tin. Heat in the oven until very hot at 200C/400F/Gas 6. Then pour in the batter and cook until golden brown and well risen.

VEGETABLE ACCOMPANIMENTS

I have given you methods only here, as the ingredients will depend on how many people are dining at your table. If you're cooking very large amounts, you need to keep an eye on the vegetables while they're cooking, and perhaps let them cook for a little longer.

ROAST POTATOES

- Peel the potatoes and cut in half lengthways.

- Place in a saucepan, cover with cold water. Bring to the boil and simmer for 5 minutes, then drain.

- Toss the potatoes in some plain flour. Heat a little oil and butter in a frying pan and fry the potatoes until golden brown in colour. Transfer to a baking tray and place in the oven for about 20 minutes at 200C/400F/Gas 6 until lovely and crisp outside, but quite fluffy inside.

ROAST PARSNIPS

- Peel the parsnips and cut into wedges lengthways.

- Place in a saucepan, cover with cold water, bring to the boil and simmer for 3-4 minutes. Drain then toss them in some Parmesan cheese.

- Place on a baking tray, drizzle over a little oil and roast for about 20 minutes in a hot oven at 200C/400F/Gas 6.

GLAZED CARROTS AND SHALLOTS

- Peel the carrots and the shallots. Cut the carrots into quarters lengthways.

- Place the carrots and the shallots into a saucepan, cover with water and simmer for 5 minutes. Drain, reserving the stock for gravy.

- Heat a little oil and butter in a frying pan. Stir in 1 tablespoon of Demerara sugar, then add the carrots and shallots and cook until they have a lovely caramelised glaze – around 3 to 4 minutes.

- Sprinkle over some chopped parsley.

BUBBLE AND SQUEAK CAKES WITH ONION MARMALADE

This is a great dish to make if you have vegetables left over after Christmas. Years ago, when I got married, we would usually have vegetables left over from our Sunday lunch, so our supper would be 'bubble and squeak'. I have updated the recipe for a new century!

Ingredients
450g/1 lb mashed potatoes
225g/8oz cooked cabbage
bunch spring onions, finely chopped
1 tablespoon chopped parsley
1 tablespoon creamed
   horseradish sauce
salt and pepper
1 egg, beaten
50g/2oz plain flour

The Onion Marmalade
450g/1 lb onions
50g/2oz Demerara sugar
150ml/¼ pint white wine vinegar
25g/1oz butter
1 tablespoon olive oil
2 cloves crushed garlic
juice and rind of 1 orange
pinch of ground cloves and cinnamon
salt and pepper

Method

- Mix all the leftover vegetables together in a large bowl. Add the spring onions, the parsley, the horseradish sauce, the seasoning and the egg. Bind all the ingredients together and divide into about 6 cakes.

- Season the flour with salt and pepper, then toss the cakes in the seasoned flour.

- Heat a little oil and butter in a frying pan, and fry the cakes for 2-3 minutes until golden brown on both sides.

- To make the onion marmalade: thinly slice the onions.

- Heat the butter and olive oil in a heavy-based saucepan. Then stir in the onions, the cloves and cinammon, and the garlic. Gently cook until soft.

- Pour in the vinegar, the orange juice and rind, and boil until the juices have become thick. This should take about 15 minutes. Season to taste.

- Serve 2 cakes per person, and arrange the onion marmalade on top.

- Garnish with a green salad.

- Tip: use any soft leftover vegetables in equal proportions, according to your taste.

GINGER CAKE

If you like the taste of ginger, then this is the cake for you. It is mouth-watering, with pieces of Chinese stem ginger giving it a luxurious texture. It can be served as a pudding with cream, or relax and enjoy a slice with a glass of port. It also makes a change from the traditional Christmas cake.

Ingredients
225g/8oz unsalted butter
110g/4oz golden syrup
110g/4oz soft brown sugar
350g/12oz self-raising flour
2 teaspoons ground ginger
150g/5oz Chinese stem ginger, cut into pieces
1 tablespoon ginger syrup
4 eggs
juice of ½ an orange

Method
- Grease and line a 20cm/8" cake tin.

- Cream together the butter, sugar and syrup until light and fluffy.

- Beat in the eggs one at a time, then fold in the flour, the ground ginger, half the stem ginger, the ginger syrup and the orange juice.

- Spoon the cake mixture into the tin, and place the remaining stem ginger on top of the cake.

- Cook in the oven on the middle shelf for 1¼ hours at 170C/325F/Gas 3 until firm to the touch. Cool in the tin for half an hour, then turn out on to a cooling tray and remove the lining paper.

- Drizzle over some ginger syrup from the ginger jar.

LUXURY MINCEMEAT ALMOND SLICES

Making mince pies can be time-consuming – these can be made in one go and kept until you need them.

Ingredients
225g/8oz plain flour
½ teaspoon mixed spice
75g/3oz ground almonds
75g/3oz caster sugar
175g/6oz unsalted butter
2 egg yolks
rind of 1 orange
1 450g/1 lb jar mincemeat

The Topping
175g/6oz unsalted butter
1 orange
50g/2oz golden caster sugar
175g/6oz plain flour
110g/4oz ground almonds
2 medium eggs, separated
1 teaspoon almond essence

Method

- Cream the butter and sugar until light and fluffy. Beat in the egg yolks.

- Stir in the flour, the ground almonds, the spice and the orange rind. With your hand bind the ingredients together until they resemble a ball of marzipan. Chill for 15 minutes.

- Roll out the pastry on a clean surface, lightly dusted with flour until it is large enough for a 30cm x 20cm/12" by 8" loose-bottomed flan tin, or a 20cm/8" round flan ring.

- Bake blind for 10 minutes at 180C/350F/Gas 4. Remove the beans and greaseproof paper. Spoon the mincemeat over the pastry base.

- To make the topping: cream the butter and sugar, and beat in the egg yolks. Stir in the flour, the ground almonds and the almond essence.

- Beat the egg whites to soft peaks, then fold into the mixture and spread over the mincemeat. Decorate with glacé cherries and angelica.

- Bake the slice for about 25 minutes at 180C/350F/Gas 4, until firm to the touch and golden in colour. Leave to cool and dust with icing sugar. Then cut into slices and serve with *crème fraîche* mixed with the orange rind and juice.

Vegetarian Winter Dinner

SPICY LENTIL SOUP

January is the time of year when we all love hot soup – ideal for a starter or for lunch, served with lovely warm crusty bread and cheese. This is a cheap and simple soup to make, but it has a hearty texture and a distinctive flavour.

Ingredients
225g/8oz red lentils, washed and drained
1 large onion, finely chopped
2 cloves garlic, crushed
3 teaspoons hot curry powder or Thai hot red curry paste
110g/4oz carrots, chopped
1.45l/2½ pints vegetable stock
salt and pepper
1 tablespoon olive oil
50g/2oz Welsh butter
3-4 tablespoons chopped chives, parsley and coriander, mixed

Method
- Heat the oil and butter in a large pan. Fry the onion, the garlic and curry powder or paste until the onion is soft.

- Add the lentils, the carrots and the stock. Bring to the boil and simmer for 20-25 minutes.

- Blend until smooth in a food processor or a liquidiser. Season to taste.

- Mix in the herbs and serve in warmed soup bowls, with warm crusty bread and some grated cheese.

CHESTNUT, LEEK AND CRANBERRY RING

This recipe is ideal as a centrepiece at any time during winter and the festive season, and it can be prepared a day in advance. Even non-vegetarians will enjoy it!

Ingredients
3 large leeks
1 large red onion
1 chopped red pepper
4 cloves crushed garlic
450g/1 lb cooked, peeled chestnuts,
    tinned or fresh
225g/8oz cranberries
175g/6oz fresh white breadcrumbs
2 tablespoons finely chopped parsley
3 eggs, beaten
450g/1 lb Cox's apples, coarsely grated
175g/6oz crumbled goat's cheese, or soft cheese
110g/4oz chopped mushrooms
50g/2oz butter
to garnish: cranberries, rosemary and bay leaves

Cranberry Sauce
450g/1 lb cranberries
225g/8oz soft brown sugar
275ml/½ pint port
275ml/½ pint orange juice
rind of 1 orange

Method

- Heat the butter in a large frying pan, and gently fry the mushrooms, the onion and the garlic.

- Finely chop the chestnuts and place in a large mixing bowl with the onion mixture, the cranberries, the breadcrumbs, the parsley, the apples, the seasoning and the beaten eggs. Mix well.

- Trim and cut the leeks down the centre, remove each leaf, wash, then place in a saucepan of boiling water and cook for 1-2 minutes. Drain, then place in cold water. Drain again and pat dry with kitchen paper.

- Grease a 24cm/9½" Savarin ring mould with butter, then line the mould with the leaves of the leeks overlapping each other.

- Place half the mixture into the leeks in the mould, and sprinkle the crumbled cheese (or spread the soft cheese) over the mixture. Add the remaining chestnut mixture and press well down. Bring the leek leaves over the top to close, leaving no gaps.

- Cook for 45-50 minutes at 200C/400F/Gas 6,and allow to cool, then turn out on to a serving plate and garnish.

- To make the sauce: put the ingredients in a saucepan and bring to the boil. Simmer for 15 minutes until the sauce is thick in consistency.

- Serve with fluffy roast potatoes and the sauce.

WARM PEAR PUDDING WITH COCONUT CUSTARD

This pudding is wonderfully comforting in the winter with a taste of apricot jam and pears. It is served with a lovely smooth coconut custard (see page 92).

Ingredients
6 fresh pears, ripe but firm, or 2 x 400g/14oz tins of pears
juice and rind of 1 lemon
4 tablespoons apricot jam
cocktail cherries
110g/4oz butter
110g/4oz caster sugar
2 eggs
110g/4oz self-raising flour

Method
- Peel the pears, then cut in half and remove the core. Poach in a pan with a little water and lemon juice for 10 minutes, then drain.

- Grease and line a 20cm/8" cake tin, spread the apricot jam over the bottom, then arrange the pears flat side down on the jam.

- To make the topping: cream the butter and sugar to dropping consistency. Now beat in the eggs, sieve the flour and fold in. Add the lemon rind. Mix to a smooth sponge.

- Spoon the sponge over the pears, cook in the oven for 15-20 minutes until the sponge is firm to the touch and golden brown at 180C/350F/Gas 4.

- Leave in the tin for 5 minutes, then turn out onto a serving plate.

- Decorate with the cherries and serve with the Coconut Custard or fresh cream.

COCONUT CUSTARD

This custard is simply delicious, especially if you like the flavour of coconut.

Ingredients
1 400ml/12fl oz tin of coconut milk
3 egg yolks
50g/2oz caster sugar
1 tablespoon cornflour

Method
- Heat the milk in a heavy-based saucepan.
- Whisk together the egg yolks, the sugar and the cornflour, then pour in the milk and whisk well.
- Pour the custard back into the saucepan and gently bring to the boil until the custard thickens. It should coat the back of a wooden spoon.

Bread Selection

TIPS FOR BAKING THE PERFECT LOAF

- Always use fresh strong bread flour. This is made especially to support the risen dough.

- Use easy-blend dried yeast for a quick and easy way to make bread.

- Make sure the liquid, usually water, is tepid or lukewarm. If it's too hot it can destroy the yeast, and if it's too cold, it causes a slow reaction in the dough.

- Add the water all at once to ensure a stretchy, elastic dough. Added gradually, it causes a tight, hard dough that won't rise.

- Knead thoroughly until the dough is smooth, elastic and no longer sticky. Use a food mixer or processor to save time.

- Always cover the surface of the dough with oiled clingfilm, polythene or a dry tea towel. This keeps it moist and allows even rising. A skinned top inhibits the risen dough.

- Always let the dough rise in a naturally warm place with no draughts. If it's in a cool place, it will take longer to rise.

- Always bake in a hot preheated oven to make the dough rise, kill the yeast to prevent further action, and cook the dough evenly throughout.

- Cool on a wire tray so that the bread stays crisp.

BASIC WHITE AND BROWN BREAD

Makes: 2 x 450g/1lb loaves
Preparation time: 15-20 minutes, plus rising period
Cooking time: 20-25 minutes

Ingredients
900g/2 lbs plain strong white or brown flour
1 teaspoon salt
1 teaspoon caster sugar
2 teaspoons oil
1 sachet easy-blend dried yeast, or 25g/1oz fresh yeast
725ml/1½ pints tepid water
beaten egg or milk, to glaze
flour to dust

Method
- Sift the flour, the salt and the sugar into a large mixing bowl. Rub in the butter with your fingertips until the mixture resembles fine breadcrumbs. Add the yeast. Stir until well blended.

- Add the water all at once. If using brown flour, you will need slightly more than if using white. Mix using your hand.

- Turn out on to a lightly-floured surface and knead well for 5-8 minutes until smooth and elastic. Alternatively, put in a food mixer or processor with dough hooks for 3-4 minutes.

- Place the dough in a clean bowl. Cover with a towel and leave in a warm place to rise for 10 minutes.

- Preheat oven to 220C/425F/Gas 7.

- Grease two 450g/1lb or 1 x 900g/2lb loaf tins, and dust with flour.

- Knead the dough again until smooth and elastic. Cut in half if making two loaves.

- Knead the dough until smooth, then roll out into an oblong. Fold both edges into the centre, then fold again.

- Place the dough in the tin, or tins, and cover with a clean towel.

- Leave in a warm place to rise until just above the top of the tin(s).

- Brush the top of the dough with egg or milk. Dust with flour and wheat or bran flakes, if desired.

- Bake in the centre of the oven until well risen and golden brown. Loosen the bread from the tin and tap the base. It should sound hollow if the bread is cooked through.

- Place bread on a wire tray and allow to cool.

VARIATIONS ON WHITE AND BROWN BREAD

Before shaping, add one of these flavourings to the risen dough. Knead until evenly blended.

110g/4oz grated cheese of your choice
1 onion, chopped and sautéed in butter
2 tablespoon chopped herbs and 1 crushed garlic clove
walnuts and 50g/2oz sun-dried tomatoes or chopped olives

MALTED GRANARY BREAD

Full of flavour and full of goodness, this loaf is a traditional favourite.

Makes: 2 loaves
Preparation time: 15-20 minutes, plus rising period
Cooking time: 20 minutes

Ingredients
900g/2 lbs granary flour
2 teaspoons salt
25g/1oz butter
1 sachet easy-blend dried yeast, or 25g/1oz fresh yeast
1½ tablespoons malt extract
500ml/18fl oz tepid water
granary flour

Method
- Place the flour, the salt and the butter in a mixing bowl. Rub in the butter finely with your fingertips.

- Stir in the yeast until evenly blended, then add the malt extract and the water all at once. Mix to form a dough.

- Turn out onto a floured surface. Knead for 5-8 minutes until elastic or use a food mixer or processor with dough hooks for 3-4 minutes.

- Place the dough in a clean bowl, cover with a clean tea towel and leave for 10 minutes.

- Preheat oven to 220C/425F/Gas 7. Grease and lightly flour two baking sheets.

- Knead the dough again for 1-2 minutes until soft and elastic. Cut in half.

- Shape the dough into two rounds and place each on a baking tray.

- Cover and leave to rise until doubled in size.

- Sprinkle the top of each loaf with granary flour. Bake for 20 minutes until well risen and golden brown.Tap the base of the loaf – it will sound hollow when cooked.

- Cool on a wire tray.

CIABATTA

This is a quick recipe for a wonderful Italian bread made with olive oil.

Makes: 3 loaves
Preparation time: 15-20 minutes
Cooking time: 20 minutes

Ingredients
900g/2 lbs plain flour
2 teaspoons salt
2 teaspoons caster sugar
2 sachets easy-blend dried yeast, or 50g/2oz fresh yeast
425ml/¾ pint tepid water
110g/4oz sun-dried tomatoes in oil, drained and chopped **or** pitted black or
green olives
2 tablespoons pesto sauce
salt and flour to dust

Method
- Sift the flour, the salt and the sugar into a large bowl, then stir in the dried yeast.

- Add the oil and the water all at once and, mixing with your hand, knead to form a dough.

- Turn out onto a lightly floured surface. Knead for 5-8 minutes until the dough is smooth and elastic or use a food mixer with dough hooks for 3-4 minutes.

- Cover the dough and allow to rise in a warm place for 40 minutes until doubled in size.

- Knead the dough for 1-2 minutes until smooth. Cut into 3 pieces.

- Add the olives or the sun-dried tomatoes to one piece, and knead lightly until evenly distributed. Shape into an oval and roll out to 30cm/12" long and 10cm/4" wide.

- Place on a floured baking tray and brush with oil. Cover with a clean tea towel and leave for 20-30 minutes until doubled in height.

- Meanwhile, repeat to make a plain loaf. Place on a tray with the sun-dried tomatoes or olive loaf.

- Roll out the third piece to 30cm/12" long and 10cm/4" wide. Brush with pesto sauce.

- On the dough, mark out three sections lengthways, so that the loaf is divided into thirds. Fold the two outer thirds over the middle section to make an oblong loaf. Brush with oil, then replace on the tray. Cover and leave to rise for 20-30 minutes.

- Preheat the oven to 200C/400F/Gas 6.

- Brush the loaves with oil. Sprinkle with salt and dust with flour. Bake for 15-20 minutes until browned. Tap the bases – they will sound hollow when cooked.

- Cool on a wire tray.

CORNBREAD

These shaped cornbreads can be baked in special moulds or made in bun tins.

Makes: 10
Preparation time: 10 minutes
Cooking time: 15 minutes

Ingredients
110g/4oz plain flour
110g/4oz yellow cornmeal
1 tablespoon baking powder
1 teaspoon caster sugar
25g/1oz butter, melted
2 eggs, size 2
250ml/8 fl oz fromage frais
6 sun-dried tomatoes in oil, drained and chopped
1 tablespoon fresh chopped chives

Method
- Preheat oven to 200C/400F/Gas 6. Place moulds or bun tins in the oven to heat.

- Sift the flour, the cornmeal, the baking powder, the salt and the sugar into a large bowl. Stir until evenly mixed.

- In a separate bowl, whisk 2 tablespoons of melted butter with both eggs and the fromage frais. Stir into the flour mixture and beat to a smooth batter.

- Remove the tins from the oven and brush with some of the remaining butter. Fill five moulds with the bread batter until rounded. Bake for 15 minutes until risen and firm to the touch.

- Turn the cornbreads out on to a wire tray. Brush the moulds with butter and return to the oven for 2 minutes.

- Add the sun-dried tomatoes and the chives to the remaining batter and stir until blended.

- Fill the moulds and bake as before. Serve warm with soup, cheese or pâté.

MUESLI BREAD

Use shop-bought muesli, or make your own, using a mixture of oats, bran and wheat flakes, together with nuts and raisins in the proportions of your choice.

Makes: 2 loaves
Preparation time: 15 minutes, plus rising period
Cooking time: 20-25 minutes

Ingredients
500g/1¼ lbs plain wholemeal flour
1 teaspoon salt
1 teaspoon caster sugar
15g/½ oz butter

1 sachet easy-blend dried yeast
or 25g/1 oz fresh yeast
150g/5oz muesli
475ml/16fl oz tepid water

Method
- Sift the flour, the salt and the sugar into a large bowl. Add the butter and rub in with your fingers until the mixture resembles fine breadcrumbs.

- Using your hand, stir in the dried yeast and 110g/4oz muesli until well blended. Add the water all at once and mix to form a soft dough.

- Turn the dough out on to a lightly floured surface. Knead for 5-8 minutes until soft and elastic,or use a food processor fitted with dough hooks for 3-4 minutes.

- Return the dough to a clean bowl, cover with a clean tea towel and leave to rise in a warm place for 10 minutes.

- Preheat oven to 220C/425F/Gas 7. Oil two 450g/1lb loaf tins. Sprinkle the inside of each with some of the remaining muesli.

- Knead the dough again for 1-2 minutes until soft and elastic. Cut in half.

- Knead each piece into a round shape, then roll between your hands to extend the length to fit the shape of small, new, clean flowerpots, or loaf tins.

- Roll the dough in the remaining muesli to coat the outside, then place in each flowerpot or tin. Cover and leave to rise to the top.

- Bake in the centre of the oven for 20 minutes until well risen and golden brown.

- Run a palette knife around the inside of the flower pots or tins to loosen the bread, then invert and turn out to cool on a wire tray.

ACCOMPANIMENTS

This final chapter suggests a few accompaniments that you can combine with any of the recipes in the book. Again, they are seasonal, but many of them will keep when stored properly, so that you can enjoy them at any time of year! There's no right or wrong combination – try them out with various dishes and see which ones suit you best.

Dishes

Marrow Relish
Lemon Marmalade
Plum Jam
Ena's Elderflower Champagne (Non-alcoholic)
Fresh Apricot Conserve
Crunchy Piccalilli

MARROW RELISH

Ingredients
1.35kg/3 lbs marrow
350g/12oz plum tomatoes
225g/8oz Demerara sugar
2 onions
225g/8oz raisins
2 cloves garlic
2 teaspoons ground ginger
1 teaspoon garam masala
275ml/½ pint cider vinegar
1 small red chilli, de-seeded and sliced
salt and pepper

Method
- Cut the marrow in half and remove the skin. Finely chop the marrow into small pieces.

- Plunge the tomatoes into hot water for one minute, remove the skins and finely chop.

- Peel and finely chop the onions and the garlic.

- Into a heavy-based saucepan, place the marrow, the onions, the garlic, the tomatoes, the raisins, the chilli, the spices and the vinegar. Cover and simmer for half an hour.

- Add the sugar and simmer for a further 45 minutes. At this point the mixture should be thick. If you like a slightly smoother consistency, just mash it a little (this is how I prefer it).

- Leave to cool, then spoon into sterilised jars.

- This chutney serves well with cold meats and barbecued food, or even with stuffed marrow.

LEMON MARMALADE

Makes about 2.25kg/5 lbs

To make this refreshing marmalade, choose fresh unwaxed lemons. Marmalade is not only for breakfast, but can be used in cakes, sponges, scones, savoury dishes or added to double cream fillings. This is a sharp marmalade which has a lovely tangy taste.

Ingredients

9 unwaxed lemons
3 limes
1.35kg/3 lbs preserving sugar

1.75 litres/3 pints water
a knob of butter

You will need a piece of muslin or clean cloth

Method

- Remove the peel off the lemons and limes with a sharp knife. Don't worry if some of the pith comes off.

- Cut the peel into very thin strips.

- Cut each lemon and lime in half and squeeze out all the juice. Strain, and reserve the pips.

- Place the water in a heavy-based saucepan with the juice and rind.

- Place the lemon and lime pith into a piece of muslin together with the pips, as the pith contains a lot of pectin. Now tie the muslin to the saucepan handle and drop into the water. Bring to the boil and simmer, covered, for 1 hour.

- Remove the muslin bag and squeeze any excess juice into the pan.

- Warm the sugar in the oven for about 10 minutes. This helps the marmalade to set quickly. Pour the sugar into the lemon liquid and heat gently, stirring until it has dissolved, and add the butter. Bring to a rolling boil, and boil rapidly until the setting point is reached, about 30-45 minutes.

- To check the marmalade: put a plate in the fridge. After boiling the marmalade for half an hour, remove the plate from the fridge and place a spoonful on the plate. After a few minutes, draw your little finger through it – if it has a crinkly skin on its surface, the marmalade is ready. If not, continue to boil for a further 10 minutes.

- Remove from the heat if there is a lot of skim, and spoon off. Leave the marmalade for about 1 hour before putting into clean, sterilised jars.

PLUM JAM

September is a lovely time to think of making jam or chutney. If you have plum trees in your garden, why not make some delicious jam with no additives, which makes it healthy, and so tasty to eat.

Ingredients
1.35kg/3 lbs plums
1.35kg/3 lbs preserving sugar
275ml/½ pint water
a little knob of butter

Method
- Wash the plums in cold water, then cut the plums in half and remove the stones.

- With the knob of butter, grease the pan. This prevents the jam from sticking.

- Place the plums into a large, heavy saucepan or a preserving pan, with the water. Bring to the boil and boil for 15 minutes.

- Stir in the sugar and gently simmer until all the sugar has dissolved, then boil rapidly for about half an hour, stirring at intervals until the jam is at setting point.

- To check the jam: put a plate in the fridge. After boiling the jam for half an hour, remove the plate from the fridge and place a spoonful of the jam on the plate. After a few minutes, draw your little finger through it – if it separates, the jam is ready!

- Allow to cool slightly and spoon or pour into clean, sterilised jars.

ENA'S ELDERFLOWER CHAMPAGNE
(Non-alcoholic)

When my friend Undeg rang me asking for a recipe for elderflower champagne, I tried out some old recipes I had, but I wasn't really happy with any of them. I decided to experiment and make up my own recipe. This is my version, which is delicious and most refreshing. It is quite exciting picking the elder-flowers during the months of May and June before the berries appear.

An added advantage is that my recipe contains no additives. Should you wish to make cocktail drinks, add a little Cassis or Campari to the champagne, or your preferred fruit liqueur.

Ingredients
12 large heads of elderflower, or 24 small ones
450g/1 lb white lump sugar
juice and peel of 4 lemons
4.5l/1 gallon water
2 tablespoons white vinegar

Method
- Place the elderflower heads, the sugar and the lemon juice and peel into a large enamel bowl (Pyrex or earthenware are also suitable).

- Boil the water, let it cool slightly and pour over the elderflower. Stir in the sugar. Add the vinegar, and mix until the sugar has dissolved.

- Cover and leave for 2 or 3 days.

- Strain the champagne into clean, dry, screw-top bottles. Store in a cool place for up to 3 months.

- Tip: should you wish to keep the champagne for a long period of time, before straining, stir in half a Camden tablet, available from your local chemist. WARNING: IF YOU SUFFER FROM ASTHMA, DO NOT USE!

FRESH APRICOT CONSERVE

This conserve is delicious served with hot scones, a freshly-made sponge cake, or on a slice of freshly-baked bread.

Ingredients
900g/2 lbs apricots, fresh or ready-to-eat
900g/2 lbs granulated sugar or preserving sugar
juice of 1 lemon
a knob of butter
275ml/½ pint water

Method
- Halve the apricots and remove the stones. Crack the stones with a nut-cracker and remove the kernels. Blanch in boiling water for 2 minutes, then drain and dry them, removing the skins.

- The kernels have an almond flavour, and if you wish to add them to the conserve, chop them finely and set aside.

- Grease the base of your preserving pan with a little butter, and add the apricots, the sugar, the lemon juice and the water.

- Slowly bring to the boil, making sure that the sugar has dissolved.

- When the sugar has dissolved, turn up the heat and boil rapidly for 10-15 minutes.

- To test: pour a little mixture on to a cold plate and allow to cool for a few minutes. Then draw your finger through it. If a crinkly skin has formed, the jam is ready; if not, boil for a few more minutes then carry out another test.

- To remove any skim at the end, add a little knob of butter. Add the chopped kernels if you wish, and pour the conserve into warm, clean jars. Seal the jars whilst still warm.

CRUNCHY PICCALILLI

Makes 1.35kg/3 lbs

This piccalilli is delicious served with ham, or a variety of cold meats, or indeed simply with cheese and crusty fresh bread. So why not make it!

Ingredients
350g/12oz small runner beans cut into 2.5cm/1" lengths
1 large cauliflower, divided into florets
2 large onions, roughly chopped
450g/1 lb courgettes, cut in half then chopped
1 red pepper, de-seeded and finely chopped
40g/1½ oz sea salt
1 tablespoon ground turmeric
1 tablespoon wholegrain mustard
2 teaspoons ground ginger
25g/1oz cornflour
2 cloves crushed garlic
225g/8oz Demerara sugar
1 red pepper
570ml/1 pint white pickling vinegar

Method
- Place all the prepared vegetables into a large bowl. Sprinkle them with salt, cover them with a cloth and leave overnight.

- The following day rinse under cold water, then drain.

- Pour the vinegar into a heavy-based pan, bring to the boil, then add the turmeric, the ginger, the mustard, the cornflour, the garlic and the sugar. Simmer until the sugar has dissolved.

- Add the vegetables and cook for 10 minutes. The vegetables should still be slightly crunchy when ready.

- Cool, then pour into clean, dry jars. Cover with non-metallic lids.

- This will keep for about six months.